garden
style
ideas

Better Homes and Gardens® Books
Des Moines, Iowa

Better Homes and Gardens® Books
An imprint of Meredith® Books

Garden Style Ideas
Editor: Vicki L. Ingham
Contributing Editor: Jilann Severson
Art Director: The Design Office of Jerry J. Rank
Copy Chief: Terri Fredrickson
Copy and Production Editor: Victoria Forlini
Editorial Operations Manager: Karen Schirm
Managers, Book Production: Pam Kvitne, Marjorie J. Schenkelberg
Contributing Copy Editor: Julie Cahalan
Contributing Proofreaders: Becky Danley, Beth Lastine, Nancy Ruhling
Indexer: Beverley Nightenhelser
Electronic Production Coordinator: Paula Forest
Editorial and Design Assistants: Kaye Chabot, Karen McFadden, Mary Lee Gavin

Meredith® Books
Publisher and Editor in Chief: James D. Blume
Design Director: Matt Strelecki
Managing Editor: Gregory H. Kayko
Executive Editor, Home Decorating and Design: Denise L. Caringer

Director, Operations: George A. Susral
Director, Production: Douglas M. Johnston
Executive Director, Sales: Ken Zagor

Vice President and General Manager: Douglas J. Guendel

Better Homes and Gardens® Magazine
Editor in Chief: Karol DeWulf Nickell

Meredith Publishing Group
President, Publishing Group: Stephen M. Lacy
Vice President-Publishing Director: Bob Mate

Meredith Corporation
Chairman and Chief Executive Officer: William T. Kerr

Chairman of the Executive Committee: E. T. Meredith III

contents

Garden-style decorating is about bringing indoor comfort to the outdoor spaces you migrate to when warm weather arrives. Whether your outdoor living space is the front porch, a back deck, a three-season sunroom, or a detached gazebo, make it personal and inviting. Furnished with comfy seating, handy

outdoor rooms

tables and footstools, and pots and planters brimming with flowering plants, your outdoor space may become your favorite room. When decorating for outdoor living, look for exterior-grade materials designed to withstand the elements. Vintage items may need to be used in sheltered areas or given a coat of matte-finish marine varnish for protection.

Surround a covered outdoor space with blooms of every sort. Pots and planters border the floor, climbers add color to columns, and a stenciled pattern of vines and flowers rings the ceiling. To make a large, rambling border even wider, use two rows of the stencil. After the outer design is in place, add another row, offsetting the pattern and allowing the designs to overlap slightly.

overheadgarden

1. **Fill the nail holes and other imperfections in the ceiling.** Sand the ceiling and wipe it clean with a tack cloth. Paint the ceiling with the base coat color.

2. **Measure the ceiling.** If desired, break it into several small areas instead of one large design area. Using the size of the stencil as a guide, determine the width of the outer border. If the ceiling has regular grooves or seams such as the beadboard ceiling shown *opposite*, use these lines as an edge for the border. After the base coat is dry, mask off the outer border using low-tack painter's tape. Seal the tape to the ceiling with a plastic card. Paint the outer border. Remove the tape.

3. **After the wide outer border dries,** add one or two narrow inner borders in the same manner using contrasting colors.

4. **Spray the back of the stencil** with adhesive according to the manufacturer's directions. Starting in the least conspicuous corner, press the stencil into place. (If using stencil cream or crayons, follow the manufacturer's directions.) Load the stencil brush with color. Blot and scrub it onto a paper plate to remove most of the paint. Using a pounding motion, tap the paint through the stencil opening. Without moving the stencil, paint all of one color before switching to the next color.

5. **When the entire motif is stenciled,** carefully peel away the stencil and move it to the adjacent spot and paint in those colors. Repeat this process until the entire border is stenciled. To form the corners, use either part of a stencil and then turn it to continue the motif or place the stencil on the diagonal.

6. **Allow the paints to dry for several days.** If desired, seal the paint with clear exterior sealer.

>TIP Breaking a large ceiling into several smaller segments as shown *opposite* makes an oversized area seem less expansive and the pattern more dominant. Clean the back of the stencil before moving to the next area. **>TIP** For this project, choose paint made especially for stencils. Stencil creams or crayons work well and are less messy when you're stenciling on an overhead surface.

You'll Need
> *Wood filler*
> *Sandpaper*
> *Tack cloth*
> *Latex paint in the desired colors for the ceiling base coat, outer border, and one or two inner borders*
> *Paintbrushes*
> *Tape measure*
> *Purchased precut stencil*
> *Low-tack painter's tape*
> *Rigid plastic card such as an old credit card*
> *Spray-on stencil adhesive*
> *Stencil brushes*
> *Stencil paints in the desired colors*
> *Paper plates*
> *Water-based exterior sealer (optional)*

Catch a few winks and a bit of a breeze at the same time. It's easy to create a bed that gently rocks you to sleep—simply use a standard twin-size box spring and mattress, a basic wooden frame, and hardware designed for porch swings. Choose a spot that isn't likely to be pelted with rain; protect the box spring and mattress with zip-on vinyl covers.

naptimeswing

❯**NOTE** Most twin-size box springs and mattresses measure approximately 36×75 inches, but sizes may vary slightly from brand to brand. Because of the weight of the frame and bed, do not use a bed larger than twin size.

1. **Measure the size of the box spring.** Cut a 2 × 4 board 2 inches longer than the length of the head of the box spring and a matching piece for the foot of the box spring. Cut two side rails, each 2 inches shorter than the length of the box spring.

2. **Working on a flat surface,** lay out the above boards into a frame. The top and bottom pieces should extend 1 inch beyond the side rails to accommodate the screw eyes. See the photograph *opposite* for detail.

3. **Glue and screw the frame together,** making sure the pieces butt together perfectly. While the glue dries, cut four cross-rail pieces to fit between the side rails.

4. **Slide the cross-rail pieces** between the side rails, placing them parallel to the top and bottom rails and spacing them evenly. If necessary, gently tap them into place with a hammer so they are flush. Glue and screw them in place. Sand all the pieces. If desired, seal the wood with exterior wood sealer.

5. **Measure in 1 inch** from each end of the top and bottom rails. Drill holes to receive the screw eyes at these spots. Insert the screw eye, add a washer, and tighten it with a nut.

6. **Lay the frame on the floor** directly under where it will be suspended. A sturdy beam should fall directly over the lengthwise center of the frame. Measure straight up to the beam and mark the position of the hanging hooks. Do not place the hanging hook in the ceiling or roof. Drill a pilot hole and insert the hooks into the beam.

7. **Thread heavy chain from one hook,** down to the frame and through a screw eye, across the frame through the other screw eye, and back up to the hook. The chain should form a triangle and elevate the frame a few inches off the floor. See the photograph *opposite* for details. Repeat for the other end of the bed. Use a level to make sure the frame hangs evenly.

8. **Lay the box spring and mattress in place.**

You'll Need

❯*Twin-size box spring and mattress*
❯*Tape measure*
❯*2 × 4 pine lumber (exterior grade is best, especially for severe climates)*
❯*Saw*
❯*Wood glue*
❯*Wood screws*
❯*Hammer (optional)*
❯*Sandpaper*
❯*Exterior wood sealer (optional)*
❯*Paintbrush (optional)*
❯*Drill and bits*
❯*4 large eye screws with matching washers and nuts*
❯*2 large hooks for hanging porch swings*
❯*2 lengths of heavy-duty chain for hanging swings (the length will depend on ceiling height)*
❯*Large level*

Place a traditional Shaker peg rack outdoors to create a hanger that is both functional and decorative. Vintage tools and a straw garden hat appear ready for use whether they are a part of a collection hung simply for their aesthetic value or actually put into use. Bundles of herbs and flowers and a freshly made wreath add texture and color while they dry in the warm summer air.

naturaldisplay

You'll Need
›*Purchased Shaker peg rack kit (should include screws)*
›*Exterior wood sealer (optional)*
›*Paintbrush (optional)*
›*Tape measure*
›*Level*
›*Drill and bits*
›*Wood glue*

1. If you want the rack to keep a new look, seal it with exterior wood sealer. To let it weather, leave the wood untreated.

2. Determine where the rack will hang. If the rack will be used for drying herbs and flowers, place it in a spot protected from excessive sun and wind. Hold the rack in place and straighten with a level. ›**NOTE** If the rack hangs on a wall with strong horizontal lines such as the one shown *opposite*, align it with the lines of the wall instead of parallel to the ground. Mark spots for pilot holes. Drill small pilot holes.

3. Hang the rack according to the manufacturer's directions. For some racks, the screws are countersunk and hidden under pegs. For others, the screws go through countersunk holes and are covered with plugs.

4. Glue the pegs in place.

›**TIP** To dry flowers and herbs, cut them at the peak of their bloom. Bind the stems together with rubber bands. As the stems dry and shrink, the rubber bands will keep them together. (Twine or wire will not pull in as the stems shrink, and the bundles will loosen.) Cover the rubber bands with garden twine, leaving long loops for hanging from the pegs. Hang the bundles upside down and allow the plants to dry naturally. This may take from several days to several weeks depending on the moisture content of the plants and the humidity.

Add the interest of a rug to your deck floor without the worry of slipping and tripping or the hassle of bringing it indoors in inclement weather—paint it in place. Use two related colors of semitransparent deck stain to keep the pattern from being too bold. Keep the shape simple, too. Diamonds are shown here, but stripes or squares would work just as well. A wide border around the outer edge defines the space and gives a finished look.

diamonddeck

1. **Measure the desired size** of your painted rug. Draw this dimension onto graph paper. Mark the outer border, then draw the diamond design within the border. Make any adjustments necessary so the measurements are easy-to-follow increments.

2. **Check the deck for raised nails** and pound them back in place. Wash and treat the deck according to the directions on the label of the solution. Lightly sand the area to be painted and wipe it clean with a tack cloth.

3. **To transfer the design from the graph paper** to the deck, start by making one corner with a T square. Measure across to the other corner of the same side and snap a chalk line. Repeat for the remaining sides. See photograph A.

4. **Measure in from the outer chalk lines** and snap four additional lines to create the border.

5. **Referring to the graph-paper pattern,** mark the diagonal lines that will form the diamonds. Snap chalk lines to create these lines.

6. **Run a utility knife blade** along the chalk lines. Use the T square or other straight edge to keep the lines perfectly straight. The groove created by the blade will keep the stain from bleeding into the next section.

7. **Beginning at the center,** paint alternating diamonds with stain. See photograph B. After the diamonds dry, paint the remaining diamonds with the second color. When all the diamonds are dry, paint the outer border.

8. **If desired,** seal the entire deck with deck sealer.

You'll Need
❭ *Tape measure*
❭ *Graph paper*
❭ *Pencil*
❭ *Hammer (optional)*
❭ *Deck-washing solution*
❭ *Sandpaper*
❭ *Tack cloth*
❭ *T square or corner square*
❭ *Chalk line and chalk*
❭ *Utility knife*
❭ *Semitransparent deck stain in two colors*
❭ *Disposable foam brushes*
❭ *Deck sealer (optional)*

Dress a potting shed, garage, or garden cottage with a simple and graphic design. Purchased bamboo trellises provide a structure for fast-growing blooming vines or a base for staking tall, spindly plants. The uncovered areas of the trellis offer an interesting pattern that changes as the sun moves and shadows fall. Place the trellises several inches from the structure to allow for air circulation and to prevent painted or brick surfaces from being damaged by plants, humidity, or mildew.

bamboo trellis wall

1. Stretch out the trellises to cover the entire wall of the building. To join several trellises, overlap the bamboo legs and lash them together with twine at several spots.

2. Measure out from the wall 6 or more inches along the overhang and drill pilot holes to receive the screw hooks. Insert the screw hooks for hanging the trellis. Tie the trellis to the hooks with twine, making sure it is opened out evenly.

3. Anchor the lower edge of the trellis to the ground with long hook bolts or U-shape stakes.

4. Trim the trellis away from windows and doors using heavy-duty pruners or a small saw. **❯TIP** For maximum impact, cover the entire wall with trellis, lashing together as many trellises as needed to cover the area. Trim the trellis from windows and doors. To plant a moss-lined planter or window box, see page 97.

You'll Need
❯*Purchased bamboo trellises*
❯*Twine*
❯*Tape measure*
❯*Drill and bits*
❯*Large screw hooks or hook bolts*
❯*Long hook bolts or U-shape stakes*
❯*Heavy-duty pruners or small saw*

A

You'll Need

> *Etching pattern, opposite*
> *Paper*
> *Window with clear glass*
> *Vinegar*
> *Rags or paper towels*
> *Clear contact paper*
> *Tape*
> *Crafts knife*
> *Etching cream*
> *Old paintbrush*
> *Disposable gloves*
> *Protective eyewear*
> *Sponge*
> *Decorative hooks or screw eyes for hanging*
> *Fabric, rope, cord, or wire for hanging*

Framed glass with a simple etched design adds a bit of privacy and interest to an open space, but still lets the view show through. Use one or more of these windows above a porch rail, in front of a screened area, or even as a window treatment. Commercial etching cream makes the process easy and safe. Use a salvaged window or mount new glass in a frame of stock molding.

glass etchings

1. Trace the pattern *below right* onto paper. If necessary, adjust the size to fit your window using a copy machine with enlarging capabilities.

2. Wash the window with soapy water. Rinse the glass with equal parts of vinegar and water to remove any residue. Dry the glass thoroughly.

3. Tape the pattern to the wrong side. See photograph A.

4. Apply clear contact paper to the right side of the window, covering the design area and several inches beyond the pattern on each side. To apply the contact paper, peel away a small section of the backing and smooth the sticky side to the window. Smooth the contact paper to the glass with your hand. If the contact paper wrinkles, lift it up and smooth it back into place. Continue peeling away the backing as you press the remaining contact paper in place. After the backing is removed, smooth the contact paper in place so it is tightly bonded to the window.

5. Using a crafts knife, cut along the design lines of the pattern. If you make a mistake, press the contact paper back in place and recut the line. If there are gaps in the mistakes, patch that area with a scrap of contact paper.

6. Peel away the contact paper from the cutout areas. See photograph B. If the edges are not tightly adhered to the glass, run your fingernail over them. Check the cutout areas for fingerprints and, if necessary, wipe those sections with the vinegar-and-water solution. Dry the glass.

7. Following the manufacturer's directions, paint etching cream onto the cutout areas. See photograph C. ⟩NOTE Etching creams contain strong chemicals. It is best to wear disposable gloves and protective eyewear.

8. After the etching cream has worked for the recommended time, rinse it away with a sponge and plenty of water. This can be done outside with a hose. Remove the remaining contact paper. Wash and dry the window.

9. Insert decorative hooks or screw eyes in the upper edge of the frame to hang the window.

*quicktricks

Add the feel of outdoor walls without closing yourself in. Movable screens made from salvaged materials, lush plants, and garden architecture define a space and create privacy.

Garden Room Archways and other garden architecture abound at garden centers and home improvement stores. Make the entrance to a garden sitting spot grander by adding a pre-made arch. If a fence and gate exist, place the archway just inside the gate to create the feel of a foyer.

Shutter Wall Hinge together long window shutters to create a tall wall for complete privacy or to block the sun. Identical panels may fit together more easily, but mismatched pieces add

privacy please

interest. If old shutters are not available, look for inexpensive new ones at home improvement centers. Make sure the bottom edges of the shutters align perfectly, and join the panels with at least three sets of double-action hinges following the package directions.

Plain Panes Break the view into smaller segments and make it feel more intimate with old mullioned windows. Join two or more windows with double-action hinges. Make sure the bottom edges of the windows align perfectly so they are steady. Use two or more pairs of hinges per joint, depending on the size of the window. For safety, consider removing the glass or replacing it with screen.

Dividing Plants Line up pots and plants of all different sizes to shape the outer edge of a garden room. Potted trees, trellises, and tall shrubs provide height, while shorter plants leave a window-like opening. Best of all, these walls may be moved as your mood or the season changes.

The livin' is easy and breezy when rooms are decked in garden decor. Floral prints, garden artifacts, and a bright, airy feel invite you to live with a summery attitude no matter what the weather or season. Like the outdoor areas that inspire them, some garden-style rooms reflect an old-fashioned flower patch packed with color,

indoor rooms

pattern, texture, and visual treats; others assume the formal, controlled, and slightly restrained look of well-manicured hedges and beds. Most fall somewhere in between. The most successful garden-style rooms depend on three things: patterns and textures reminiscent of the outdoors, actual garden elements, and good light.

The look may be painterly, but the technique couldn't be easier. An abstract trellis and stylized roses require only the most basic brush strokes. Use a wide, bold design like the one shown here as a wainscoting pattern for a large room. In a smaller room, reduce the size of the design by using a narrower brush and reducing the pattern. Tone down the colors a bit, and you can cover entire walls.

painted trellis

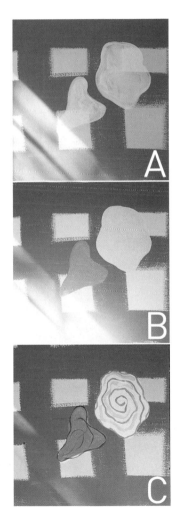

1. If you need to change background colors, base coat the wall the desired color. This should be lighter than the trellis color. Be sure to make any repairs in the wall before painting.

2. Divide the wall into a large grid for the trellis pattern. The grid can be slightly uneven. Use a level or a tape measure to keep the horizontal lines parallel to the floor and the vertical lines at right angles to the horizontal lines. Lightly mark the lines with a pencil or chalk line.

3. Using a 3-inch-wide brush (narrower for a smaller trellis) and following the lines, paint the trellis pattern. The lines can be slightly uneven and rough along the edges.

4. While the trellis paint dries, enlarge or reduce the rose and leaf patterns *above* to the desired size. Trace the flower pattern onto the wall. For interest, rotate the pattern or vary it slightly for each flower. Trace a leaf close to each flower.

5. Using white acrylic paint and a medium artist's brush, fill in each flower and leaf shape. See photograph A.

6. Paint the leaves green and the roses with the light flower color. See photograph B. **❯NOTE** It may take several coats to cover the trellis paint.

7. Using a narrow artist's brush and the darker flower color, paint around the outside edge of a rose. The outlining should be loose and uneven and does not have to follow the exact shape of the flower. To indicate rose petals, paint a loose and uneven spiral from the center of the rose to the outside edge. Use the spiral on the pattern as a guide only. Repeat the outlining and petal details for all the roses. See photograph C.

8. Using a narrow artist's brush and the darker green paint, outline the leaves in the same manner. Add a few random veins to each leaf, using the pattern as a guide only.

You'll Need

❯ *Latex paint for base coat*
❯ *Paint roller and brush for base coating (optional)*
❯ *Level*
❯ *Tape measure or yardstick*
❯ *Large level or chalk line*
❯ *Pencil*
❯ *Heavy paper or lightweight cardboard for patterns*
❯ *Scissors*
❯ *3-inch-wide paintbrush*
❯ *Latex or acrylic paint for trellis design*
❯ *Acrylic crafts paint in white, light and dark green (for leaves), desired flower colors (each flower needs a light and a dark color in the same hue)*
❯ *Medium-size artist's brushes*
❯ *Narrow artist's brush*

Bring the serenity of a walk in the woods into your bedroom. A screen made from bifold doors acts as a headboard and, when decorated with reverse-stenciled leaves, takes on the look of a forest floor.

woodlandscreen

You'll Need

> *Bifold doors (enough to go across the head of the bed when hinged and folded to stand securely)*
> *Double-action hinges (optional)*
> *Screwdriver*
> *Sandpaper*
> *Tack cloth*
> *Latex primer*
> *Paintbrush and roller*
> *Paint roller pan*
> *Several leaves in different sizes and shapes*
> *Stencil plastic*
> *Narrow-tipped permanent marker*
> *Clear tape*
> *Self-healing cutting mat or piece of glass*
> *Crafts knife*
> *Light green latex paint for the background and darker green latex paint for the foreground*
> *Latex glaze*
> *Small foam paint roller for glazing*
> *Clean lint-free rags*

>NOTE The screen shown *opposite* is made from preassembled narrow bifold doors. To cover a large space, use two or more sets of doors or choose full-size hollow-core doors and join them with hinges.

1. **Remove the hinges from the doors.** Sand the doors and wipe them with a tack cloth. Prime all the surfaces of the doors, then paint them with one or more coats of the base color. Sand lightly between each coat of paint.

2. **If the leaves do not lie flat,** place them between pieces of newspaper and press them between heavy books for a few days. They do not have to dry. Photocopy the leaves, enlarging or reducing them as desired.

3. **Place the leaf photocopies on a flat surface.** Lay a piece of stencil plastic over each leaf shape and trace the outline with a narrow-tipped permanent marker. Tape the stencil plastic to a self-healing cutting mat or piece of glass. Cut along the outline with a crafts knife. If you make a mistake, tape the slit back together and cut again.

4. **Mix equal parts of dark green paint and glaze.** Starting at the top of one door and working in two-foot sections, place a leaf template on the door and roll over it with the paint/glaze mixture. See photograph A *opposite* for details. Remove the leaf and put another one down. The leaves can overlap slightly. Paint over this leaf in the same manner. When working with small leaves, several may be rolled at one time. Continue until approximately 2 feet of the door are covered.

5. **Dampen a clean lint-free rag** and wring it almost dry. Roll the rag into a sausage shape. Lay the rag over the stenciled area and roll it over the images to blend and mottle them. See photograph B for details.

6. **Add leaf images** to the remaining sections in the same manner until the door is covered. As the rag becomes saturated with paint, re-roll it or change to a fresh one.

7. **Fill in bare spots** with additional leaves or glaze. Use another damp rag to blot sharp edges and blend the sections together. See photograph C. To further blend the images, rag-roll over the entire door. Wipe excess glaze from the edges of the door. Repeat for each door.

8. **Put the doors back together** with their original hinges. If you are using more than one set of doors, join them into one large panel using additional hinges or simply stagger them slightly. To join sets of doors, set them on the floor in their final positions. Make sure they are secure and level. Place three double-action hinges between each set of doors. Mark their placement and attach the hinges to the doors following the directions on the package. >TIP If your floors are uneven or heavily carpeted, the doors may tip easily. Fold the doors at tight angles to make them more stable. To further stabilize them, cut several 6-inch sections of 1 × 2 lumber. Cut each section diagonally to form two wedges. Sand and paint the wedges to match the base color of the doors. Nail the wedges to the bottom of each door to act as legs that will help keep the doors from tipping. Alternate sides so both the front and back of the screen are stabilized.

A

B

C

Embellish unadorned neutral-color linens with a simple painted design. Look for 100-percent-cotton sheets with a high thread count (200 threads per inch or more).

woodlandlinens

1. Machine wash and dry the linens that are to be painted. Do not use detergent with additives or add fabric softener in either the washer or dryer. Iron the sections to be painted so they are smooth and wrinkle-free.

2. Trace the leaf pattern *below* onto heavy paper or cardboard, adjusting the size as needed to fit the border of your linens.

3. Measure the width of your linens and determine the placement of the leaves. The designs shown *opposite* start approximately 3 inches from the outer edge and are spaced about 1½ inches apart. Tape the sheet or one of the pillowcases to the work surface so it is smooth and flat. ❯**TIP** To keep the paint from bleeding through and make your painting surface smoother, slip a piece of poster board between the layers of the pillowcase.

4. Using a pencil or fabric marker, lightly trace the leaves onto the linens in the desired spots. Draw an S shape between each leaf. See photograph A for details.

5. Mix the textile medium and acrylic paint according to the directions on the textile medium bottle. This will help the fabric better receive the paint and make the paint softer, more permanent, and less prone to fading.

6. Using a fine-tipped artist's brush, paint along the design lines. Repeat for the remaining linens. See photograph B for details.

7. Heat-set the paint according to the textile medium manufacturer's instructions.

A

B

You'll Need
❯*100-percent-cotton white or neutral-color bed linens*
❯*Steam iron*
❯*Heavy paper or lightweight cardboard for pattern*
❯*Tape measure*
❯*Low-tack painter's tape*
❯*Poster board*
❯*Soft lead pencil or fabric marker*
❯*Textile medium to mix with acrylic paint*
❯*Acrylic paint to match the screen or room colors*
❯*Container for mixing paint*
❯*Fine-tipped artist's brush*

Plain bed frames take on the romance of an English garden when fence posts and pickets form the head- and footboards. The new wood is whitewashed for an aged look, and hinges and handles are added just for fun. To complete the look, bold floral paper covers the walls.

picket fence beds

1. Measure the ends of the bed frame. The newel or porch posts should fit at the outer edge of the frame. Use this same dimension to determine the length of three pieces of 2×4 lumber that form the structure at each end. Calculate the total number of 2×4 boards needed and the number of pickets required for each end. The 2×4 across the top of the pickets and between the posts will be shorter.

2. Measure the desired height of the newel posts (with finials) and the pickets. This will vary depending on your taste, the height of the frame, and the depth of the mattress. Note that on the headboard shown, the pickets are tallest in the center and graduate down in size toward each end.

3. Cut the boards to size.

❯NOTE A home improvement center can do this for you at a minimal charge. Be sure to have your measurements with you and mark the order and placement of each piece as it is cut.

4. Lightly sand the pieces to remove splinters, leaving the pickets slightly rough. Wipe them clean with a tack cloth.

5. Dilute the paint with water until it is the consistency of cream. Paint each piece. Before the paint dries, wipe away the excess with a rag to leave a whitewashed finish.

6. Glue and nail the posts to the ends of the three 2×4s at the head of the bed and the 2 long 2×4s at the foot of the bed. The ends of the 2×4s should align with the outer edges of the posts. See the photograph *opposite* for details.

7. Turn the above pieces so the 2×4s lie against the floor. Glue and nail the pickets in place, spacing them evenly. Fill the nail holes and touch up with paint.

8. Turn the headboard and footboard upright. Glue the remaining 2×4 across the top of the pickets on the footboard. See the photograph *opposite* for details.

9. Attach the headboard and footboard to the bed frame with screws. (There should be openings in the frame to allow for this. If the screw head is too small and slips through the hole, place a washer between the frame and the screw head.)

10. Glue the finials in place. If desired, add a handle and hinges to create the look of a gate. **❯TIP** The materials shown were left in their rough state for an aged look. For a smoother finish, purchase better-quality pickets and sand them until they are smooth. Use a diluted wash as described *above* or a crackle finish medium from the paint department to achieve the aged look. For a new look, paint the smooth pickets and posts with two or more coats of paint.

You'll Need

- ❯ Bed frame
- ❯ Tape measure
- ❯ Saw
- ❯ Sandpaper
- ❯ Paintbrushes
- ❯ Clean rags
- ❯ Wood glue
- ❯ Hammer
- ❯ Nails
- ❯ Wood filler
- ❯ Drill and bits
- ❯ Screws for attaching the frame to the headboard and footboard (size varies with the openings on the frame)
- ❯ Washers (optional)

Plus, for each bed:
- ❯ 2×4 boards cut the width of the bed frame; see the instructions for details
- ❯ Pickets (9 were used on each end of a twin-size bed shown right, but the number will vary with the bed size, picket size, and spacing)
- ❯ 4 porch or newel posts
- ❯ Latex paint
- ❯ 4 finials to top the posts
- ❯ Fence handle and hinges (optional)

Evoke a summertime mood year-round with dragonfly table linens. To keep sewing to a minimum, use linen pillowcases for the chair backs and cut up a bed sheet to make the chair seats and table runner. The neutral colors shown here give the room an elegant look, but bright hues would work just as well and lend a whole different feeling to the room.

stenciled dragonfly
table linens

You'll Need

❯ Pillowcases and flat sheet in linen or 100-percent-cotton
❯ Water-erasable fabric marking pen
❯ Tape measure
❯ Sewing scissors
❯ Seam ripper
❯ Sewing machine
❯ Sewing thread to match the bed linens
❯ Steam iron
❯ Poster board or cardboard to fit a pillowcase
❯ Paper for pattern
❯ Fine-tipped permanent marker
❯ Stencil plastic
❯ Tape
❯ Self-healing cutting mat or piece of glass
❯ Crafts knife
❯ Textile medium for acrylic paint
❯ Acrylic paint
❯ Scissors
❯ Paper plate
❯ Stencil brushes

1. Machine wash and dry the linens that are to be painted. Do not use detergent with additives or fabric softener in either the washer or dryer.

2. Slip a pillowcase over a chair back so the closed end fits the top of the chair back snugly. The pillowcase will be longer than the chair back and bunch up at the seat. Mark the spot where the side seam of the pillowcase meets the seat of the chair. See the photograph *opposite* for details. Remove the pillowcase from the chair.

3. Measure from the hemmed edge of the pillowcase up to the mark. Mark this same point on both sides of each pillowcase. If both sides of the pillowcase are seamed, open out the seams to the marked points. If only one side is seamed, open the seam to that point. On the opposite side, slash the pillowcase open to the mark. Narrowly hem the opened edges on both sides of the pillowcase.

4. Measure your table for the proper size runner, adding the desired drop to each end and ¾ inch on each side for hems. ❯**NOTE** that the table runner shown *opposite* has the top band of the sheet used as one decorative edge. Turn the raw edges under ¼ inch and then ½ inch and topstitch the hem in place.

instructions continued on page 32

instructions continued from page 31

5. For the seat covers, measure across the seat from side to side and add the desired drop measurement to each side. Measure the seat from front to back and add the same amount of drop in the front. Add 1¼ inches to each edge for the hem. Cut rectangular seat cloths to fit these measurements from the remaining fabric. Turn under the raw edges ¼ inch, then turn under a 1-inch hem. Topstitch the hem in place close to the folded edge.

6. Press the fabric pieces so they are smooth and wrinkle-free. To make the pillowcase fabric smoother and keep the paint from soaking through, slip a piece of poster board or lightweight cardboard into the pillowcase.

7. Trace the dragonfly pattern onto paper, adjusting the size of the pattern *left* as desired. Tape stencil plastic over the pattern. Trace the outline of the dragonfly with a fine-tipped permanent marker.

8. Tape the stencil plastic to a self-healing cutting mat or piece of glass. Using a sharp crafts knife, cut out along the outline. Remove the cutout pieces.

9. Mix the paint and textile medium according to the directions on the bottle of textile medium. Textile medium will keep the paint softer, help it adhere to the fabric better, and make it more permanent.

10. Tape the table runner to your work surface, making sure the fabric is taut but not distorted. Photocopy or trace several of the dragonfly motifs and roughly cut them out. Place the patterns on the table runner, spacing them as desired. Remove one pattern and replace it with the stencil. Dip the tip of the stencil brush into the paint mixture. Pounce it onto the paper plate to remove almost all the paint. Tap the brush onto the fabric through the stencil openings. Use a pounding motion to force the paint into the fabric. See photograph A.

11. After the entire motif is stenciled, carefully remove the stencil. See photograph B. Clean off the stencil and move it to the next pattern and repeat the process.

12. Stencil the table runner and each chair back and seat cover. Heat-set the paint according to the textile medium instructions. **❯TIP** When cutting a stencil, use plastic made especially for stenciling. If your knife slips when cutting, tape over the mistake with clear tape, sealing it tightly to the plastic. Apply tape to the top of the stencil only. Recut the stencil on the proper line.

Walls painted with widely spaced stripes and simplified flowers convey an innocent, old-fashioned mood when topped with a coat of antiquing glaze. The flowers shown here were done freehand, but the pattern provided makes painting easier for the inexperienced artist. Use the pattern as it is shown or modify it slightly for each motif.

flowers&
stripesglazing

You'll Need

❯ *Eggshell-finish latex paint for the base coat*
❯ *Paintbrush and paint roller*
❯ *Paint roller tray*
❯ *Tape measure*
❯ *Plumb line or level and yardstick*
❯ *Chalk line (optional)*
❯ *Pencil*
❯ *1-inch-wide paintbrush*
❯ *Latex or acrylic paint for stripes*
❯ *Heavy paper or lightweight cardboard for templates*
❯ *Scissors*
❯ *Acrylic crafts paint in green and at least three other colors for the flowers*
❯ *Artist's brushes*
❯ *Small containers for paints*
❯ *Black paint pen*
❯ *Antiquing glaze or clear glaze and umber-color paint*
❯ *Clean, lint-free rags*

1. Paint the wall with two coats of the base color. Make sure you have filled holes and sanded rough spots before painting.

2. Measure the walls and divide them into even increments for the stripes, spacing the stripes 24 to 32 inches apart. ❯**NOTE** The stripes may be placed closer together, but part of the design's charm is that they are widely spaced. Use a plumb line or level and yardstick to make sure the lines are straight and parallel. Lightly mark the lines with a pencil or chalk line.

3. Using a 1-inch-wide brush, paint each stripe. Leave breaks in the stripes large enough to accommodate the flower design *above*. Be sure to stagger the breaks in the lines so the flowers fall at different points on adjacent stripes.

4. Trace the flower designs *above* onto heavy paper and cut them out. Hold the patterns to the wall and lightly trace around them.

5. Paint each design using the desired color and an appropriately sized artist's brush. See photograph A. For a painterly look, leave a few brushstrokes and let some of the background color show through. ❯**TIP** For a bolder look, use two or more coats to make the flowers solid.

6. Using a paint pen and following the manufacturer's instructions, draw around each flower and leaf. Add curves in the roses to indicate petals and dots in the centers of the other flowers. See photograph B. Let the paint dry.

7. For an aged look, lightly rub antiquing glaze over the entire wall. Use a premixed antiquing glaze or mix your own glaze by combining equal portions of clear glaze and umber paint. Dampen a rag with water and wring it out. Dip it into the glaze and rub the glaze down the walls, leaving a slightly streaked effect. See photograph C. Replace the rag as it becomes saturated.

A keen eye can spot potential tables in the oddest places. Simply look for any flat, stable surface that fits your space and needs. With little or no adaptation, you'll have an unusual desk, side table, or even a dining surface.

*quick**tricks**

Birdbath Magazine Table Create a perfect catchall space with a sculptural birdbath. Whether used for magazines and books or as a place to stash mail, keys, or other everyday items, the birdbath keeps clutter under control. Make sure the top and bottom are securely attached. If necessary, use epoxy glue to hold them together. If you prefer a flat surface, place a piece of glass over the birdbath. Before having glass custom-cut, check home decorating and accessories stores to see if they carry precut rounds of glass, which may be less expensive. Place decorative items such as stones, dried flowers, or seashells in the birdbath and lay the glass over the top.

table talk

Sawhorse Desk These former carpenter's tools moved to an office job. With the addition of a glass top, weathered sawhorses become a clean, modern desk. Set the sawhorses in place, then measure for the size of the top. You will want the glass to extend beyond the sawhorses several inches on each side. Contract a glass shop to cut ½-inch-thick glass for the top; have the edges smoothed and the corners rounded slightly. (These are often called "dime corners" because they are rounded to about the size of a dime.) Place the glass over the sawhorses. If you wish, place clear plastic "bumpers" (available at hardware stores) between the sawhorse tops and the glass to keep the glass from slipping and scratching.

Stepladder Side Table Give a small stepladder a good scrubbing, then put it to work as a side table or plant stand. Check the legs for signs of dry rot and the hinges for tightness and make sure the ladder stays even and steady when you apply slight pressure. If the top is stained or worn beyond your taste, cover it with a doily or linen napkin. The steps provide ideal display areas, while the top holds larger items such as plants, beverages, books, remote controls, or even the telephone.

Wash Bench Coffee Table A weathered outdoor bench serves as the perfect coffee table for a small, narrow space. Clean the bench thoroughly and use a wire brush to remove loose or flaking paint. Old paint may contain lead, which could be toxic if ingested. The dust also contains lead, so mist the surface with water before scraping loose paint to control the dust. If small children or pets are in the home, consider sealing the bench with matte-finish polyurethane to keep paint from flaking. This may decrease its value, but it will be less likely to continue losing paint.

When you're looking for garden-style items for your home, the hunt is half the fun. After combing through your basement and attic, expand your search to flea markets, garage sales, and antiques shops. And don't forget to peruse the curbside. The key to garden-style collecting is to use your imagination and see an

finding
garden treasures

item for what it can be, not for what it is right now. A wash bench can become a coffee table, an old fence can take the place of a bulletin board, and a wire basket can store towels and bath products. If just the right item is nowhere to be found, look to reproductions. They're often less expensive, easier to work with, and will stand everyday wear better than antique pieces.

Use an old window frame to create a new view. Hang a single mullioned window or a matched pair on the wall and use the compartments to display plates, photographs, and other small mementos. Make sure the glass is removed and the frame is sturdy. Brush away old caulk and flaking paint with a wire brush. (Always wear a dust mask when working with old paint.) To repair broken mullions, join the pieces with a small amount of wood glue and clamp them in place until the glue dries.

windowshelf

You'll Need
> Old window frame(s)
> Small molding strips or dollhouse trim (optional)
> Small handsaw (optional)
> Paint to match the window frame (optional)
> Paintbrush (optional)
> Wood glue (optional)
> Small clamps (optional)
> D- or triangular-shape hanging rings
> Hammer
> Pencil
> Small nails
> Picture hooks

1. The mullion strips of many windows have small ridges for holding the glass in place. They also keep plates, photographs, and other items from slipping in the same manner a plate rail works on a shelf. If your window does not have ridges, install a small rail in the front of the mullions to act as a barrier to keep the displayed items in place. Cut narrow molding strips or doll-house trim to fit the inside dimensions of the pane area. Paint the strips to match the frame. Glue and clamp the strips in place. Remove the clamps after the glue is dry.

2. Nail hanging rings on the back of the frame near the upper corners. Hold the frame in place and mark the spots where the tops of the rings meet the wall. Remove the frame and set it aside.

3. Attach the picture hooks to the wall at the marked points. Check the hook package to make sure the hooks are large enough to hold the weight of the frame.

4. Hang the frame from the hooks. Arrange your display as desired. If the hook tops show, paint them to match the wall.

Variation on a Theme Old wire garden edging creates another simple display. Determine the length of edging that will fit the wall and join or disassemble the panels as needed. Hang the edging on the wall using small finish nails. ❯TIP To help prevent plaster from flaking, stick a piece of low-tack painter's tape to the wall where the nail will be placed. Drive the nail through the tape at a slight downward angle, then carefully peel the tape away. Tuck photographs, postcards, notes, or other flat items between the wires.

You've filled your room with wonderfully aged garden items, painted and glazed the walls for old-world charm, and created enchanting vignettes from outdoor odds and ends. The room is the epitome of well-blended garden style with one exception. The fireplace surround with its fine finish and dark color becomes an unwanted focal point because it doesn't fit the subtle colors and well-worn textures that fill the rest of the room. The solution is easy. Strip the varnish and treat the surround to a faux finish that looks like weathered wood.

weathered wood

You'll Need
❯*Heavy plastic drop cloths*
❯*Low-tack painter's tape*
❯*Paint or finish stripper appropriate for the original finish*
❯*Paintbrushes*
❯*Protective eyewear*
❯*Rubber gloves and mask appropriate for paint stripping*
❯*Fine-grade sandpaper*
❯*Tack cloth*
❯*Latex paint to match the room*
❯*Paint crackle medium (optional)*
❯*Old lint-free rags*

1. **Place heavy drop cloths** on the floor, hearth, and any other surface and tape off the walls around the fireplace surround to protect other surfaces from the paint stripper.

2. **Apply the paint stripper and remove the finish** according to the manufacturer's directions. Be sure to wear protective eyewear, gloves, and a mask and work in a well-ventilated area. Some spots may take more than one application.

3. **Sand the wood and wipe it clean** with a tack cloth.

4. **Dilute the paint with water** until it is approximately the thickness of cream. Paint the wood using uneven strokes.

5. **After the paint dries, sand areas** that would have received the most wear—any edges and corners, the top, or places likely to have been touched or bumped often. Sand some spots down to the bare wood and sand others lightly. See the photograph *opposite* for details.

6. **If a crackled alligator finish is desired,** paint the wood with commercial crackle medium and another coat of paint following the manufacturer's directions for the crackle medium. ❯**TIP** This same technique may be used to age other wood surfaces such as furniture, baseboards, floors, and new wood accessories. For an even more subtle color, dilute the paint with an equal amount of water. Apply the paint with a brush and then wipe most of it away with a clean, lint-free rag. This technique is sometimes called pickling.

Mock up your own version of garden-style wallpaper by covering a wall with vintage botanical prints, pages from garden journals, or old seed packets. Look for old paper memorabilia with garden motifs at flea markets and antiques shops or check garden centers and catalogs for reproductions. For a successful arrangement, keep items similar in color and style. Arrange them randomly, in straight lines, or even checkerboard fashion, but keep them close together for the most impact.

botanicalwalls

1. **Trim the pages or make copies of the images** so they are all the same size. If you are working with flat images, they can be enlarged or reduced on a color photocopier or by scanning and printing on a computer. To reproduce the garden journal collage shown *left*, press and dry flowers and glue them to paper. For instructions on pressing flowers, see page 67.

2. **Place the pieces** in identical picture frames. If the pages are matted, use matching mat board.

3. **Hang the images evenly and closely** together so the wall is covered. Mark where the picture hangers will be placed, then nail each hanger to the wall before hanging. To keep the frames from shifting, check framing departments for small self-adhesive rubber bumpers that stick to the back of the frames at the lower corners.

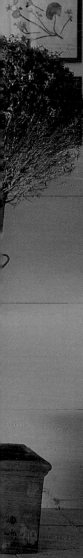

You'll Need
> *Pages from a garden journal or botanical book, all the same size and style (see the directions for details)*
> *Matching frames*
> *Picture hangers*

Variation on a Theme For a casual arrangement of garden images, tack seed packets to a wall. Look for vintage seed packets or choose reproductions from garden centers and catalogs. For the most unified arrangement, choose packets that are similar in color and style and look to be about the same age. Place them on the wall in a pleasing arrangement. Avoid having identical packets next to each other and balance the arrangement so items with dense designs are interspersed with those having a more open image. Hold them in place with a pushpin or thumbtack that blends with the seed packet background. If your wall does not accept pushpins, use removable double-stick adhesive designed for hanging posters.

Recycling old outdoor containers and other items adds storage space as well as interest to a plain bathroom. Wire bins, old hooks, and an aged ladder take on the job of holding towels and other essentials while keeping the room looking open and airy. A small chair steps in for a side table. Here it holds a bouquet of fresh flowers, but it could just as easily stash extra towels and grooming accessories for guests.

creativestorage

You'll Need
> *Vintage storage pieces such as wire bins, window boxes, ladders, hooks, and chairs*
> *Soap or cleanser*
> *Scrub brush*
> *Paint or clear sealer (optional)*
> *Paintbrush (optional)*
> *Tape measure*
> *Level*
> *Awl*
> *Hammer*
> *Picture hooks, mirror clips, screw eyes, fine wire, and other mounting and hanging supplies (will vary with each project)*
> *Screwdriver or cordless drill and screwdriver bits*
> *Needle-nose pliers*

1. Thoroughly clean the storage items to remove dirt, old paint, or debris. If desired, give them a fresh coat of paint or clear sealer. The humidity of a bathroom may cause metal items to rust and bleed onto the wall if not sealed.

2. To hang a wire rack, measure to center it in the proper position. Mark spots for picture hangers, making sure they are level. Make pilot holes with an awl and hammer the picture hangers into the wall. Hang the upper wire of the basket from the hangers. If desired, use pliers to wrap the V-shape end of the hanger around the top of the basket to hold it more securely in place.

3. To keep the lower edge of the basket from pulling away from the wall when used, mount mirror clips under it so they fit over the lower wires.

4. Secure a ladder to the wall by using two or more pairs of small screw eyes and fine wire. Set the ladder in place. Mark points on the wall directly behind the upper rung and close to each upright.

5. Make a pilot hole above and below each of the marked points. Insert a screw eye at each of these spots. Wrap wire around one screw eye, loop it over the rung of the ladder, and pull it tightly through the other screw eye. Tie off the wire and clip the ends. Repeat for the other side of the ladder. This will keep the ladder from slipping or tipping as towels or other items are removed.

6. To use old hooks on a door, hold them in place and mark through the hanging holes. On a paneled door, be sure to hang the hooks from the thicker part of the door and check the length of the screws to make sure they do not go completely through the door. Make a pilot hole at each of these points. Replace the hook and drive the screws into the door.

7. If a screw does not match the hardware, dab a bit of paint over it so it blends with either the hardware or the background.

Well-worn statuary brings an established feel to a garden but is becoming harder to find and pricier as it becomes more collectible. Instead of spending years searching for the perfect figure, take the easy way out. Visit local ornament dealers, then add a painted finish to give your piece an antiqued look. Roadside stands, farmers' markets, and flea markets often offer the best selection at the lowest prices. Don't shy away from pieces with a small flaw. It only adds to the character and aged appearance.

aging concrete

You'll Need
> *New cast concrete garden statue or figure*
> *Latex or acrylic paint in off-white and caramel colors*
> *Paintbrush*
> *Clean, lint-free rags*
> *Clear semigloss spray sealer*
> *Latex or acrylic glazing liquid*

> **TIP** Old statues often have bits of fine moss growing on them. This may take years if done naturally. To hurry the process, paint the crevices of the figure with uncultured yogurt or buttermilk (check health food stores for milk products without cultures). Take small sections of moss and dirt with moss spores from the ground, trees, or old pots. Rub the moss and dirt into the yogurt or buttermilk. Spray the moss with liquid plant food. Keep the moss or dirt moist. For the best results, place the statue in a cool, damp, and shaded area. This method is successful about half the time, and it may still take several months before the moss grows to the concrete, depending on the humidity, temperature, and type of moss.

1. **Paint the concrete with off-white paint,** brushing the paint on and then rubbing it into the concrete.

2. **Spray the figure with sealer** to protect the concrete from the elements and keep the base coat from flaking. See photograph A for details. After the sealer dries, apply a second coat of off-white paint in the same manner.

3. **Mix 3 parts of caramel-color paint** with 1 part of glazing liquid. Adjust the color as needed by adding paint, glaze, or additional colors.

4. **Dampen a rag, then wring it out.** Dip a small portion of the rag into the glaze mixture, picking up a small amount of paint. Rub the glaze onto the concrete, leaving the color slightly uneven. Continue until the figure is covered with glaze. See photograph B for details.

5. **Let the paint dry.** Add additional caramel-color glaze to any recessed areas to add depth. The figure *opposite* is darker around the eyelids, in the curls of the hair, and in the crevices of the fabric and wheat.

6. **Mix equal parts of off-white paint** and glazing liquid. Rub this paint mixture onto areas that are raised and would receive more wear from the elements, such as the raised portions of the cloth, the top surface of the arm, and the nose on the figure *opposite*. Blend the two colors together so the change is subtle.

7. **After the paint dries,** seal it with two or more coats of semi-gloss sealer for protection.

A

B

Plastic pots hold many advantages over their clay counterparts. They're lighter in weight, less likely to chip and break, can withstand weather changes, retain moisture better to keep plantings from drying out, and often are less expensive. Although a variety of styles is usually available, the pots are most often found in one color—terra-cotta. With a little paint, that same pot can take on the look of aging lead or cast aluminum. Be sure to carry your paint technique at least a few inches down on the inside (below dirt level) so none of the original color will show even if the dirt is low.

painting plastic

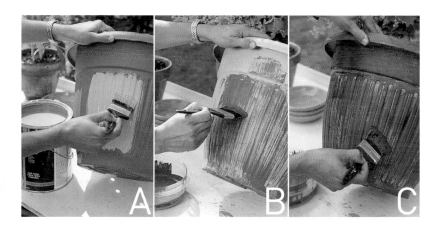

You'll Need
❯ *Plastic pot with grooves and detailing*
❯ *Fine-grade sandpaper*
❯ *Clean, lint-free rags*
❯ *Exterior latex paint in medium gray, black, and white*
❯ *Paintbrushes*
❯ *Container for mixing paint*
❯ *Paint stir stick*
❯ *Plastic wrap*
❯ *Exterior polyurethane sealer*

1. **Lightly sand the entire pot to slightly roughen the finish** and make it more receptive to paint. Wipe it clean with a clean rag or tack cloth.

2. **Paint the pot with a light coat of medium gray paint.** See photograph A. Allow the paint to dry at least four hours. Apply a second coat and allow it to dry an additional four hours. Two thin coats will provide a better base than one heavy coat.

3. **Mix 3 parts gray paint with 1 part black paint.** Stir the paint until it is slightly blended but some streaks remain. The uneven mixture will help give the pot a more authentic look.

4. **Working quickly so the streaks do not disappear,** apply a thin coat of the darker gray mixture. Allow some of the base coat to show through, especially in recessed areas. See photograph B. Let the paint dry several hours. Wrap the brush in plastic wrap so the gray paint remains in the bristles and does not dry out.

5. **Dip the tip of the brush in white paint.** Using a light touch, brush white paint into the recessed areas and along the rim to give the pot a chalky finish. See photograph C. Wipe away any excess white paint with a clean rag. Let the paint dry four hours.

6. **Apply two coats of polyurethane sealer,** letting the pot dry completely between coats.

Start with inexpensive metal watering cans, buckets, and planters, add a little paint, and voilà! You have an instant verdigris finish that mimics the treasured look of aged copper. The key to success is applying the paint in thin coats so the different layers of color show through. Look for metal pieces that have simple, basic lines. They'll not only receive the finish better, but they are also more likely to resemble old pieces that have aged naturally.

painted verdigris

1. **Wash the metal container** with a solution of 1 part vinegar to 4 parts water to remove any film. If the container is slick, lightly sand it and wipe it clean.

2. **Prime the container with metal primer.** This will help the acrylic paint adhere to the metal. Let the primer dry.

3. **Brush on a coat of gold acrylic paint,** making sure all exposed surfaces are covered. See photograph A for details. If the primer shows through, add a second coat of gold paint after the first coat dries.

4. **Mix 4 parts of umber paint with 1 part clear glaze.** Brush the umber mixture over the gold paint. Allow some of the gold paint to show through. See photograph B for details.

5. **Mix 4 parts of aqua paint with 1 part clear glaze.** Using a dry bristle brush, dip the very tip of the bristles in the aqua paint mixture. Swipe the brush back and forth across a paper plate until most of the paint is removed. Using the dry brush, haphazardly brush the aqua paint over the umber coat. Let some of the gold and umber show through and allow the brushstrokes to create an uneven texture. Do not smooth out the paint. See photograph C and the photograph *opposite* for details.

6. **After the paint dries, spray the container** with two or more coats of polyurethane sealer.

You'll Need
> *Metal container*
> *Vinegar*
> *Fine-grade sandpaper (optional)*
> *Clean lint-free rags*
> *Metal primer*
> *Paintbrushes*
> *Acrylic paint in metallic gold, umber, and aqua*
> *Containers for acrylic paints*
> *Paper plate*
> *Clear acrylic glazing liquid*
> *Matte or satin polyurethane sealer*

That perfect piece of primitive furniture may be out there somewhere, in just the right size and shape and with the right layering of mellow colors. But maybe it simply doesn't exist anywhere except in your dreams. Create your own worn and layered look by distressing an unfinished or painted piece of furniture. After you have found the furniture, look to the rest of the room for color cues for the different layers of paint.

distressedwood

›TIP For indoor furniture, use interior latex paint and sealer. If the piece will spend time outside, substitute exterior paint and sealer.

1. **Sand the furniture with fine sandpaper** and wipe it clean with a tack cloth. Paint the wood with a coat of primer.

2. **After the primer dries, add the base coat.** Let the paint dry. This will take several hours depending on humidity.

3. **Working with the grain of the wood,** rub wax over the base coat. See photograph A. Concentrate the wax on the areas that would naturally receive the most wear, such as along the edges and top surface. The wax coat should be light and slightly uneven. This will help separate the layers of color.

4. **Add a second color of paint over the wax.** See photograph B. This coat can be slightly uneven and may not adhere well in some spots because of the wax.

5. **After the paint dries,** place the furniture on a drop cloth or newspapers. Wear a dust mask and protective eyewear. Using medium-grade sandpaper, sand away portions of the top coat so the base and primer coats show through. See photograph C. Sand away more paint on the edges and other surfaces that would receive the most wear. When you have achieved the desired effect, wipe the furniture with a tack cloth.

6. **If desired, repeat the waxing and painting steps** with additional colors. Sand those layers in other areas so all the colors show.

7. **After the paint is dry,** seal the wood with two coats of polyurethane to protect the paint and make the colors richer.

You'll Need

›*Unfinished or painted furniture*
›*Fine- and medium-grade sandpaper*
›*Tack cloth*
›*Latex primer*
›*Paintbrushes*
›*Latex paint in two or more colors*
›*Solid white wax, such as an old pillar candle or a block of paraffin*
›*Drop cloth or newspapers*
›*Dust mask*
›*Protective eyewear*
›*Polyurethane sealer*

Cast-resin plaques and figures offer an abundance of possibilities to the garden-style decorator. Because they are virtually impervious to weather and wear, these ornaments are perfect for adding character to any little nook or cranny. Their neutral color can be boring, though, and even a bit jarring when placed among foliage. Soften their look and add a bit of aged character with a paint-rubbing technique.

agedresin

1. **Use a damp rag to clean the plaque and remove dust.** Let the piece dry completely.

2. **Paint the plaque with a base coat of off-white paint.** See photograph A. Let the paint dry.

3. **Mix 4 parts of green paint with 1 part glazing liquid.** Working in small sections, paint the plaque green. Tap the brush into the corners and crevices, allowing the paint to puddle a bit in these areas only. See photograph B. Use a damp rag to blot away excess paint. Repeat for the remaining sections.

4. **Using a damp rag, rub paint off the raised areas** and portions of flat areas so the finish looks worn and uneven. See photograph C. Using the same rag, rub paint into the crevices. If necessary, add paint to some sections for highlights.

5. **After the paint dries,** seal the plaque with three coats of matte-finish polyurethane sealer. Allow the sealer to dry between coats.

You'll Need
❯*Cast-resin plaque or figure*
❯*Clean, lint-free rags*
❯*Latex paint in off-white and sage green or another desired color*
❯*Paintbrushes*
❯*Latex glazing liquid*
❯*Matte-finish polyurethane sealer*

A

B

C

Cans, bottles, pitchers, and jars are the Eliza Doolittles of the vase world—untapped beauties just waiting for their chance to flower. Look around the house, garage, and attic for containers with interesting shapes, then match them to the flowers you pluck from the garden or farmer's market.

*quick**tricks**

Bottled Up Bottles old and new hold single blooms. When clustered, they take on the look of a flower bed. Look for old bottles at garage sales and flea markets. Reproduction bottles are popping up at gift shops. One of the most convenient sources is the grocery store. Check out beverage bottles as well as those holding vinegars, oils, and assorted condiments. If a bottle brush won't work to clean an old bottle, pour in a little kosher salt. Add a few drops of water, hold your hand over the opening, and shake the bottle. The abrasive salt may loosen dirt, debris, and lime. Add more water to dissolve the salt, then rinse well.

instant vases

Pitcher This Enamelware pitchers, coffeepots, and mugs are the perfect way to display a country-garden bouquet. Make sure old vessels are watertight before setting them on wood and free of rust if they will be in contact with a metal surface. Running a bead of latex caulk along the joint and pressing it into the seam with your finger can sometimes seal small leaks. If old enamelware isn't handy, check out the camping aisle of discount and sporting goods stores.

Do the Can Can Vintage cans (or those that simply look old) make the perfect containers for old-fashioned flowers. Those with paper labels may need a dab of glue to reattach the label, but one with the brand name painted directly on the tin may be used as is. To add a handle, use an awl to punch two holes opposite each other and close to the upper rim. Loop wire through one hole and pinch it back on itself. Wrap the wire around the top and through the other hole. Clip the wire and pinch it back on itself.

Door A-Jar Don't save special surprises just for May Day. Leave an unexpected bouquet on friends' and neighbors' doors any time of year. Look for jars with a wide rim at the top and enough screw-rings to keep a tie from slipping off. Wrap twine, raffia, braid, or other trim around the neck and tie it tightly. Leave one end long enough to loop and tie around the doorknob, then pack the jar full of small flowers.

Details, details, details. Attention to the little things is a vital element in decorating a room—and can be the most fun part. **Adding handcrafted items brings comfort, style, and personality to a garden-style room. Accessories such as pillows, lamps, picture frames, and plants give the room its finishing touches.**

accessories

Soft items such as pillows, plants, quilts, and window treatments take the harsh edge off hard objects such as garden ornaments, birdhouses, and outdoor furniture. Use the two—soft and hard—in tandem for the most interest. Check out garden and home improvement centers, crafts stores, and kitchen shops for raw materials sprouting with garden style.

When an old tablecloth is simply too pretty to be hidden in the linen drawer, hang it up for display. Bright, unusual, and sometimes just plain odd designs from the 1940s and 1950s make cheerful window valances. Shutters, sheers, or plain panels may be used on the lower portion of the window, or just leave it uncovered if privacy is not a priority.

valance

You'll Need
›*Square vintage or reproduction tablecloth*
›*Steam iron*
›*Spray starch (optional)*
›*Two large decorative drapery tacks*
›*Hammer or rubber mallet*
›*Old towel or rags (optional)*

›**TIP** Choose a tablecloth that is wider than the window when folded on the diagonal. The lower point should fall at least one-third of the way down the window but can go longer. If you are covering more than one window, consider using reproduction cloths so you can buy several of one pattern and match the size of the window to the size of the cloth. If you prefer a vintage cloth, choose one stunning pattern, then cover the rest of the windows in coordinating checks or stripes. Cut the fabric to the size of the cloth, narrowly hem the edges, and hang it in the same manner.

1. **Press the tablecloth to remove all the wrinkles.** To add more body, apply a light coat of spray starch according to the manufacturer's directions.

2. **Fold the cloth in half diagonally.** Center the tablecloth over the window so the fold matches the upper edge. Carefully push one drapery tack through the cloth and into the upper corner of the window frame. Hammer the tack in place. If using a regular hammer, cover the tack with an old towel to protect it from the hammering.

3. **Repeat for the other corner,** pulling the cloth taut. Fold the corners back onto themselves to form neat shapes.

Variation on a Theme Substitute architectural brackets for drapery tacks when hanging tablecloths in the window. Here a vintage wooden bracket was used, but reproduction pieces or those used for receiving a drapery rod work just as well. Mount the brackets to the wall just beyond the window frame. If the brackets do not have hanging hardware, attach sawtooth hangers to the backs. Fold the cloth in half diagonally. The one shown *at left* was loosely rolled to the diagonal midpoint instead of being folded in half like the one shown *opposite*. Slip the end of the tablecloth through the bracket. If the tablecloth slips out of place, knot it so it cannot go back through the hole, or fasten it to the wall with a pushpin that is hidden in the folds of the fabric.

Step up your style and display a collection of quilts on an old ladder. For a change of pace, hang the ladder sideways instead of upright. This not only shows off the quilts better, but it also makes a bolder statement by filling up more wall space. Let each quilt drape to a different length, making sure the most interesting part of the quilt shows. Keep the quilts out of direct sunlight to prevent wear and fading. Rotate quilts often or refold them so crease marks do not form and colors do not change because of light exposure.

ladderquiltrack

You'll Need
❯ *Old ladder*
❯ *Tape measure or level*
❯ *Pencil*
❯ *Purchased brackets deeper than the side rails of the ladder*
❯ *Paint for brackets*
❯ *Paintbrush*
❯ *Toggle bolts or similar hardware for hanging the brackets*
❯ *Screwdriver or cordless drill and screwdriver bits*
❯ *Long wood screws*

1. Measure and mark the placement of the brackets, making sure they are level. Paint the brackets with two or more coats of paint and let them dry.

2. Attach the brackets to the wall with toggle bolts or similar heavy-duty hangers. Use brackets deeper than the width of the ladder side rails to accommodate the portion of the quilt that will fall between the ladder and the wall.

3. Hang the ladder on the brackets. Check to make sure it is level. From the top, drill through the ladder side rail and into one bracket top in two places. Screw the ladder upright to the bracket. Repeat for the remaining bracket. This will keep the ladder from slipping off the brackets.

4. Fold and arrange the quilts between the rungs of the ladder, making sure they are balanced. If you prefer, substitute vintage linens, tapestries, woven or hooked rugs, or other old textiles for the quilts.

A

B

C

Preserve the look of a summer herb garden by creating small vignettes of dried herbs and flowers on wooden plaques. Whether arranged to resemble a favorite motif, such as a dragonfly, or as a reminder of gentle breezes and sweet smells, the plaques bring an aura of calmness to a corner of a room. Look for pressed and dried herbs at crafts and floral supply stores or dry your own following our suggestions *below*.

pressedherb &flowerplaques

1. **Sand the tray and wipe it clean.** Paint the entire tray with two coats of base color.

2. **To create the crackle or alligator finish,** paint the tray with crackle medium following the manufacturer's directions exactly. See photograph A.

3. **Following the directions for the crackle medium,** add a contrasting top coat of paint. For the best results, use long, even strokes and only one layer of top color. See photograph B. Add a third color to the outer rim. Let the paint dry.

4. **If desired, glue a paper doily to the tray.** Arrange the herbs and flowers on the tray. Remove the plants, keeping the same pattern. Starting with the bottom plants, paint the underside with white glue and a No. 2 artist's brush. Press the plant in place. See photograph C. Add the other plants one at a time until the design is complete.

5. **Let the glue dry.** Apply two coats of sealer.

Pressing Flowers Pick flowers and herbs at the peak of their bloom. Flat, sturdy flowers with a low moisture content will dry most successfully. Three basic types of presses may be used. Always follow the press manufacturer's directions.

1. Traditional presses. Flowers are layered between absorbent paper that's sandwiched between two boards that are pulled together by screw-type fasteners. Drying time can be from a few days to a few weeks. The flowers shrink when drying, so turn the screws on the press every few days to keep the pressure heavy and even.

2. Microwave presses. These work in the same manner as regular flower presses, but a microwave reduces the drying time. They are the most costly, and you need to work in smaller batches.

3. Do-it-yourself presses. Place the flowers or herbs on two sheets of unprinted newsprint (available at crafts stores). Place the newsprint and flowers between two books or boards or between the pages of a heavy book. Add more weight (such as bricks) to the top. Let the flowers dry completely, checking them every few days.

You'll Need
- *Wooden tray or plaque*
- *Sandpaper*
- *Clean, lint-free rags*
- *Acrylic paint in desired base, top, and rim colors*
- *Paintbrushes*
- *Containers for holding paint and glue*
- *Acrylic crackle medium*
- *Paper doily or decorative paper cut to the size of the tray (optional)*
- *Pressed dried herbs or flowers*
- *White glue*
- *No. 2 round artist's brush*
- *Polyurethane sealer*

This cute little cottage could be for the birds, but you probably will want to keep it indoors as a decorative piece. Unfinished birdhouses are available for a few dollars at garden, hardware, crafts, and home improvement stores. Pick paint colors to match your room, then follow the instructions for creating the crackle finish and "slate" roof. If you do want to place the birdhouse outdoors, give the paint a coat of matte-finish marine varnish. Make sure the roof stones are glued on with a weather-resistant epoxy or substitute wood shingles that have been painted and sealed.

tweet retreat

1. **Pound in exposed nails** with a nail punch, then fill the holes with wood filler. Sand the birdhouse and wipe it clean. Apply a coat of primer and let it dry.

2. **Paint the birdhouse with the base color.** This color will show between the crackles and on the roof and bottom edges. See the photograph *opposite* for details.

3. **Apply crackle medium to the body of the birdhouse** according

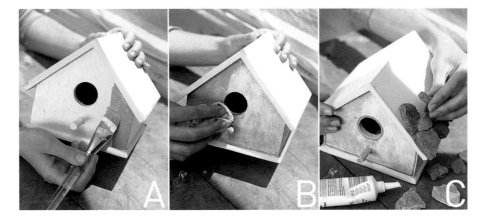

to the manufacturer's directions. Instructions vary with different brands so be sure to follow the label directions thoroughly.

4. **Using long, even strokes** and following the directions on the crackle medium, paint a top coat over the crackle medium. See photograph A. Let the paint dry. The cracks will appear as the paint dries.

5. **To give the paint an aged, chalky look,** dilute white paint with water until it is the consistency of milk. Dip a damp rag into the paint and rub it onto the birdhouse. Wipe off the excess paint. See photograph B.

6. **Seal the birdhouse** with two or more coats of clear polyurethane sealer.

7. **Starting at the bottom of the roofline,** glue stones to the roof. Overlap the stones for a shingled effect and use small stones to fill in gaps. See photograph C and the photograph *opposite* for details.

8. **Tuck a bit of dried moss** in the opening.

You'll Need
›*Purchased birdhouse*
›*Nail punch (optional)*
›*Hammer (optional)*
›*Wood filler (optional)*
›*Sandpaper*
›*Clean, lint-free rags*
›*Wood primer*
›*Paintbrushes*
›*Containers for paint*
›*Acrylic paint in two contrasting colors, plus white*
›*Acrylic crackle medium*
›*Clear polyurethane sealer*
›*Gathered or purchased small, flat stones*
›*Clear epoxy glue*
›*Small bit of dried moss*

BIRD PAINTING   VOL II   CHRISTINE E JACKSON

twig

A

Shed a little light, woodland style. A twig base styled from threaded lamp pipe, a lamp-making kit, precut wooden rounds, and twigs takes less than an afternoon to assemble. Top it off with a purchased lampshade embellished with a crumpled paper bag and leaf cutouts to carry out the natural look.

lamp&leafshade

1. Glue the two rounds together with the small one on top and the center holes aligned. After the glue dries, slide the threaded rod through the hole. Secure the rod end under the large round with a washer and locking hex nut. Secure it on top with another washer and locking hex nut.

2. Cut four ½-inch-long segments of twig and glue them to the underside for legs.

3. Bundle the twigs around the threaded rod and hold them in place with rubber bands. See photograph A for details.

4. Run several rows of tacky white glue around where you want the twine to be. Wrap the twine over the glue. Tuck the cut ends under the wrapping. Remove the rubber bands.

5. Cut small sections of twigs and glue them around the outer edge of the small round. See photograph B.

6. Assemble the lamp according to the kit instructions. The cord will run down the center of the pipe and out under the large round. One end will attach to the plug and the other will be used to join the socket to the lamp. Once the wire is in place, pull it tight and secure the end exiting from under the lamp with an overhand knot. This will help keep the wire and socket tight.

7. Cut stylized leaves from a paper bag. Spray the backs of the leaves with spray adhesive and stick the leaves to the outside of the shade.

8. Separate the inner and outer layers of a double grocery bag. Open out the inner layer. Starting at the seam of the shade, roll the shade across the bag. As you roll the shade, mark a line ½ inch beyond the top and bottom edges. Continue rolling and marking until you are ½ inch beyond the seam of the lampshade. See photograph C.

9. Cut out the shade cover. Crumple the paper, then smooth it out. Spray both the shade and cover with spray adhesive. Starting at the seam of the shade, smooth the cover over the shade. The last ½ inch should overlap the beginning line. Glue this overlap in place with tacky white glue.

10. If necessary, trim the margin at the top and bottom to an even ½ inch. See photograph D. Wrap the margin to the inside and glue it in place with tacky white glue.

11. Coat the entire outside of the shade with one or more coats of amber shellac. Let the shellac dry completely.

You'll Need

〉*Large and small precut wooden rounds with ⅜- to ½-inch predrilled center hole (available at crafts stores)*
〉*Tacky white glue*
〉*Threaded rod (also called all-thread or threaded lamp pipe)*
〉*Two washers to fit the threaded rod*
〉*Two locking hex nuts to fit the threaded rod*
〉*Adjustable wrench or wrench to fit hex nuts*
〉*Twigs*
〉*Saw or heavy-duty pruners*
〉*Rubber bands*
〉*Twine*
〉*Scissors*
〉*Lamp-making kit*
〉*Plain brown paper bags*
〉*Spray adhesive*
〉*Paper lampshade*
〉*Pencil*
〉*Amber-color shellac*

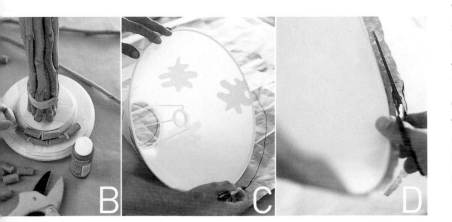

Pillows made from down-home fabrics invite everyone to snuggle up and relax a bit. The sewing is simple when using pre-hemmed materials such as towels and napkins and only slightly more difficult when cutting your own vintage or reproduction fabric. Check out the standard sizes of premade pillow forms at the fabric store and fit your pillow covers to those sizes. If you need a special size, sew a pillow insert in the same manner as the cover, pack it full of polyester fiberfill, and sew the opening shut.

You'll Need
- ❯ *Purchased or self-made pillow form*
- ❯ *Tape measure*
- ❯ *Two towels, two napkins, or fabric yardage for the cover*
- ❯ *Water-soluble or fade-out fabric marker or tailor's chalk*
- ❯ *Sewing machine*
- ❯ *Scissors*
- ❯ *Sewing thread*
- ❯ *Straight pins*
- ❯ *Zipper (optional)*

perfectpillows

Pillows Using Towels or Napkins

1. Mark the dimension of the pillow form on the right side of one of the napkins or towels.

2. With wrong sides of the two napkins or towels facing, sew three sides together on the marked line. Leave the fourth side open.

3. Insert the pillow form through the open side. Scrunch the pillow form to the opposite end and pin the opening closed along the marked line.

4. Sew along the marked line, taking care not to wrinkle the fabric underneath or catch the pillow form.

5. Shake the pillow to evenly distribute it within the form. The excess fabric beyond the stitching will form a flange edge.

Pillows Using Decorative Fabric

1. Cut a pillow front and a pillow back from fabric, cutting both pieces ½ inch larger on all sides than the pillow form.

2. With right sides facing, sew the pillow front to the pillow back on three sides using ½-inch seams.

3. Turn the cover to the right side. Insert the pillow form in the opening and slip-stitch the opening closed. These pillows will not have flange edges.

Pillows with Zippers

1. Cut the fabric ½ inch larger on all sides than the pillow form. With right sides facing, baste the front to the back along one edge using a ½-inch seam. Center the zipper along the seam line and mark the zipper stop and the zipper tab points. Sew with a regular machine stitch above and below these points.

2. **Press the seam open.** With the wrong side of the fabric up, center the zipper facedown over the seam. Unzip the zipper slightly but keep the top portion together. Pin or baste the zipper in place. Mark the tab and stop points with pins.

3. **Turn the fabric right side up.** Using a zipper foot, sew ¼ inch from the seam on both sides and across the top and bottom as marked with the pins. This will form a rectangle of stitching. Remove the basting within this rectangle. Unzip the zipper.

4. **Refold the pillow cover** so the right sides are facing. Sew the front to the back along the remaining sides using ½-inch seams.

5. **Turn the pillow cover** right side out through the zipper opening. Insert the pillow form and distribute it evenly in the case. Zip the cover closed.

Add personality plus a touch of the outdoors to plain picture frames. Look for new or old frames that have wide edges and little beveling or detailing. Add a whitewashed or antiqued finish, then top them with decorative cutouts. Look for metal shapes in crafts stores, gift shops, and architectural salvage lots. Wood and resin shapes may also be applied. Peruse the wood products aisle of the crafts store for miniature flowerpot halves, leaf shapes, tiny flat-sided watering cans, and little garden tools. Spray them with metallic paints or brush on rust-colored acrylic paint.

embellishedframes

1. Sand the picture frame and wipe it clean.

2. **Dilute white acrylic paint with water** until it is the consistency of milk. Paint the frame with the diluted paint, then wipe away the excess paint with a clean rag. If more color is desired, layer on additional coats of paint until the finish is opaque but antiqued.

3. **If desired, paint the embellishments.** Lay them out on the frame to determine their placement. For interest, let some items extend beyond the inner and outer edge of the frame. Make sure they do not interfere with the glass if the frame will be used to hold an image. If possible, nail the embellishments in place. If they cannot be nailed, glue them in place with epoxy appropriate for their material. ❯**TIP** Keep the finished frames empty and use them as sculpture or add glass, a mat, and a print or photograph.

You'll Need

❯*Wooden picture frame*
❯*Sandpaper*
❯*Clean, lint-free rags*
❯*Acrylic paint in white and any other desired color*
❯*Container for paint*
❯*Paintbrushes*
❯*Nature- and garden-related embellishments such as metal fence ornaments, tin cutouts, wood cutouts, resin figures, or miniatures*
❯*Hammer (optional)*
❯*Small brads (optional)*
❯*Epoxy glue designed for the embellishment material (optional)*

Whether you gather your twigs, branches, and pinecones from the backyard or the crafts store floral aisle, frames like these will remind you of a long, leisurely walk in the woods. Use the larger twig frame as an outer border for a smaller item such as a framed piece, a small mirror, or a wall ornament. The extra frame helps a small item make a much larger statement. Birch is traditionally used for frames like this, but this one is constructed of plain branches with a whitewash finish. The smaller purchased frame takes on a rustic look in a matter of minutes when small branches are halved, mitered, and nailed to it.

twigframes

You'll Need

❯ *Twigs or small branches*
❯ *Pruners*
❯ *White acrylic paint*
❯ *Container for paint*
❯ *Paintbrushes*
❯ *Clean, lint-free rags*
❯ *Utility knife (optional)*
❯ *Hammer*
❯ *Small finish nails*
❯ *Twine*
❯ *Pinecones*
❯ *Brown paper-wrapped floral wire*
❯ *Hot-glue gun and glue sticks*
❯ *Saw*
❯ *Purchased frame*

Large Pinecone Frame

1. Cut four twigs or small branches to the desired size. Dilute the paint with water until it is the consistency of milk. Brush the paint onto the twigs, then wipe it off for an uneven finish. Repeat until the desired color is reached. If birch is used, eliminate the painting steps.

2. Lay the twigs out into a frame shape, placing the horizontal twigs on top of the vertical twigs. If desired, make small notches in the vertical twigs to receive the horizontal twigs, fitting them together like logs.

3. Nail the frame together at the corners, using at least two nails per corner. Wrap twine over the corners to further stabilize the shape.

4. Wrap wire around the stem end of the pinecones, slipping the wire between the scales of the pinecones and twisting it tightly. Place several pinecones on each wire and join the wires into a long garland.

5. Wrap the garland of pinecones around the frame, arranging the pinecones as desired. If necessary, place a small dot of hot glue on some of the pinecones to hold them in place more securely.

Small Twig-Cornered Frame

1. Carefully cut small branches in half lengthwise. Cut the branches into four uneven pieces. Miter one end of each piece to form a corner and cut the other end straight.

2. Hot-glue the branches to a flat-surface purchased frame.

handlingtools

Turn wood-handled garden tools into stylish pulls for a gate, door, or cupboard. Drilling through the tools is the toughest part. The wood may split but the tool is still usable as long as most of the handle remains intact. New tools are less likely to split than old ones. Adding a shank behind the tool when mounting it lets you slip your hand under it without scratching your knuckles.

You'll Need
❯ *Wood-handled garden tools*
❯ *Drill and bit*
❯ *Sandpaper*
❯ *Acrylic paint in white or another desired color*
❯ *Container for paint*
❯ *Paintbrush*
❯ *Clean, lint-free rags*
❯ *Pencil*
❯ *Two narrow galvanized bolts for each tool, each long enough to go through the tool and the gate or door, plus 1⅜ inch*
❯ *Two 1-inch lengths of narrow copper pipe for each tool*
❯ *Nut to fit each bolt*
❯ *Screwdriver*
❯ *Wrench to fit nuts*

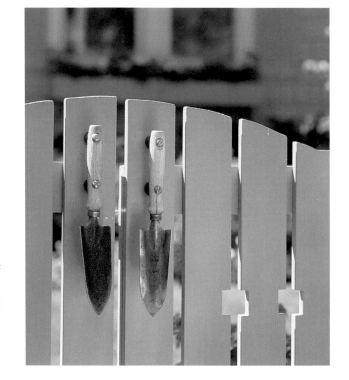

1. Carefully drill through the handle of the tool in two places, making sure not to drill into a shank that may go into the handle. Leave enough space between holes for your hand (about 2½ inches). Sand the tool.

2. Mix the paint with water until it is the consistency of milk. Paint the tool handle, then wipe away the excess paint to leave an antiqued finish. Repeat until the desired color is achieved.

3. Position the handle on the gate or door. Mark dots through the holes and drill through the gate or door at the marked points.

4. Slip a bolt through the hole in each handle, then slide a 1-inch length of copper pipe onto each bolt. Insert the bolts through the holes in the gate or door. The pipe will act as a spacer to hold the tool away from the gate or door. Thread the nut onto the bolt and tighten it.

Give It a Pull Check garden centers, home furnishings and accessories stores, and gift shops for garden-inspired drawer pulls like those shown *opposite*. Use the pulls as highlights on an otherwise plain piece of furniture. Before purchasing the pulls, make sure the spacing between screws matches that of the current handles on your furniture. If the holes do not align, you will need to fill the old holes and drill new ones. To fill the old holes, fit a dowel tightly into the hole. Cut the dowel to be flush on the front of the furniture. It can be flush or slightly indented on the inside. Pound the dowel into place. Smooth over the dowel with wood filler. When the filler dries, sand over the old holes and paint the drawer front. Drill new holes at the proper spaces.

Look to nature for alternatives to vases. A leaf-covered box filled with moss and delicate cascading flowers is reminiscent of the orchids and other flowers that grow out of stone walls and rocky crevices. The trick is to place the flowers in water-filled plastic florist's vials and add water every few days. Look for tightly capped florist's vials in the floral department of crafts stores. For the most dramatic impact, select one or two cascading blooms, such as freesia or orchids.

boxed leaves

You'll Need
❯ *Fresh galax or ivy leaves*
❯ *Heavy-duty scissors*
❯ *Newspaper*
❯ *Spray adhesive*
❯ *Papier-mâché box (available at crafts stores)*
❯ *Floral foam (optional)*
❯ *Knife (optional)*
❯ *Sheet moss*
❯ *Fresh flowers*
❯ *Florist's vials*
❯ *Small bulbs or smooth pebbles*

1. **Clip the leaves from the stems.** Lay a single layer of leaves on newspaper, wrong side up. Spray the leaves with spray adhesive following the manufacturer's directions.

2. **Spray the inside and outside of the box** with spray adhesive. Follow the suggested dry time on the adhesive label, then press the leaves to the box. Overlap the leaves and wrap them to the inside so the box is covered.

3. **For a large box,** cut floral foam to fit inside the box and within 1 inch of the top edge. For small boxes, the foam can be eliminated.

4. **Place sheet moss inside the box.** Trim the stems of the flowers and insert them through the caps of water-filled vials. Insert the vials into the foam or moss, pulling moss over the caps of the vials to conceal them.

5. **Place bulbs or pebbles on top of the moss.** Check the water level of the vials every few days and add water and fresh blooms as needed.

A coat of paint turns plastic planters into works of art with the feel of Provence. The window box and pot shown *at right* are done in pale yellow, but vibrant French blue, Mediterranean green, or a mix of colors would work as well. The designs are outlined with a gold metallic paint pen to add a bit of glimmer to catch the summer sunlight. Look to French pottery, fabrics, and dinnerware for other design ideas.

painted pots

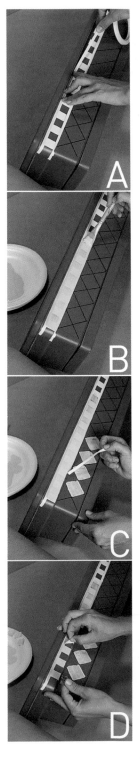

You'll Need

> *Plain-lined plastic planters and pots*
> *Denatured alcohol*
> *Clean lint-free rags*
> *Terra-cotta color enamel spray paint*
> *Square and round self-adhesive stickers from an office supply store*
> *Old credit card or similar plastic card*
> *Enamel paint in yellow and white*
> *Container for mixing paint*
> *Paintbrushes*
> *Razor blade*
> *Gold metallic paint pen*
> *Clear spray sealer*
> *Ruler*
> *Pencil*
> *¼-inch-wide graphic arts tape (available at art and office supply stores)*

For Both Pots Prepare the surface of the pot and box for painting by wiping them with denatured alcohol. Spray-paint the containers with terra-cotta color paint. This will act as a primer coat and help the decorative paint adhere better.

For the Pot

1. Apply round stickers to the body of the pot in a random pattern. Seal the sticker edges to the pot with a rigid plastic card.

2. Mix 3 parts yellow enamel paint with 1 part white enamel paint. Paint the pot with two coats of paint, brushing over the stickers.

3. After the paint dries, remove the stickers. If necessary, use a razor blade to loosen them.

4. Outline the circles with a gold paint pen. See the photograph *opposite* for details.

5. After the paint dries, seal the pot with two coats of spray sealer. Allow to dry 24 hours before planting or adding dirt.

For the Window Box

1. Measure the lower edge of the planter and divide it into even increments for the diamonds. Draw the diamond shapes onto the planter.

2. Evenly space square stickers along the top edge of the planter. Run a row of ¼-inch-wide tape along the upper and lower edge. See photograph A. Run a rigid plastic card along the tape to seal it to the planter.

3. Mix 3 parts yellow enamel paint with 1 part white enamel paint. Using a paintbrush approximately the same width as the stickers, paint over the stickers and tape. See photograph B. Add a second coat of paint after the first dries.

4. Using a small artist's brush, paint in the diamonds. See photograph C. Add a second coat after the first one dries.

5. Peel away the tape and stickers. Use a razor blade to remove the tape when necessary. See photograph D for details.

6. Outline the squares and diamonds with a gold paint pen. See the photograph *opposite* for details.

7. After the paint is dry, seal the planter with two or more coats of spray sealer. Allow the box to dry 24 hours before planting.

Don't fret over a chipped dish. Turn discarded dinnerware into handmade mosaic pots and planters. Hunt for potential art materials at garage sales, thrift stores, and junk piles. Stick to a color scheme and choose china that is all about the same thickness. Flat dinnerware such as plate rims and centers adheres to the base best. Look for patterns that will still show a design when broken into small pieces.

chinamosaics

1. **Wrap the china in an old towel** and hit it with a hammer to break it into small pieces. Be sure to wear protective eyewear and work on a surface that will not be damaged by the hammering or the broken shards. Use a tile nipper to trim the pieces to specific sizes and shapes. Make sure the shards are small enough to fit flatly against the sides of the pot.

2. **Wipe the pot clean with a cloth.** Following the manufacturer's directions, place tile adhesive on the back of the china pieces and adhere the shards to the pot. Fit the pieces together as closely as possible. See photograph A. Leave the rim undecorated or line it with contrasting china. Make sure the shards do not extend beyond the bottom of the pot and the pot sits flat. Let the adhesive dry overnight.

3. **Using a spatula,** apply pre-mixed grout between the pieces. See photograph B. Use your fingers to work the grout into small areas and

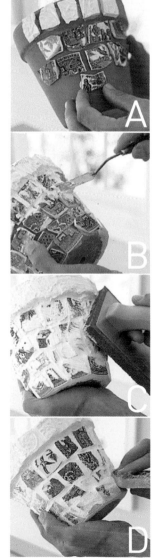

make sure it is packed tightly around the pieces. Take care when working around sharp edges and wear plastic gloves to protect your hands from both the shards and the grout.

4. **Using a grout float or heavy sponge,** smooth out the grout so it is uniformly even and comes to the edges of the shards but does not go over the edges. See photograph C.

5. **As the grout dries,** a hazy film will develop on the china. Wipe the haze away with a damp sponge or cloth. See photograph D. Do not let the film dry for more than a few hours or it may be difficult to remove and result in a hazy finish.

6. **Let the pot dry for at least a week** or until the grout dries completely. Seal the grout with commercial grout sealer. Coat the inside of the pot with two or more coats of grout sealer. This helps keep moisture from seeping into the grout from the inside of the pot. Moisture will weaken the grout and the shards may pop loose. If they do loosen, reattach and regrout them in the same manner.

You'll Need
> Old china dinnerware
> Old heavy towels
> Hammer
> Protective eyewear
> Tile nippers (often available for rent at tile and home improvement stores)
> Clay pots
> Clean, lint-free rags
> Tile adhesive
> Pre-mixed grout in the desired color
> Spatula for spreading grout
> Plastic gloves
> Grout float (also called tile float)
> Sponge
> Grout sealer
> Paintbrush

Add a little pizzazz to standard clay pots with just a few brushstrokes. Painting different pots all one color or design gives a uniform look to your container garden. For the pots shown *opposite*, wide stripes give their conical shape the fun feel of a circus tent. Choose a stripe and brush width to match your pot size. The wider the stripe, the more pronounced the V-shape of the unpainted spaces will be, making the pot look even more tapered. For other designs, look to the paint and children's sections of crafts stores for sponges or flexible stamps that can wrap around the pot.

paintedterra-cotta

1. **Sand the pots lightly** to remove rough areas. Wipe the pot clean. ❯**NOTE** It is better to use new pots for painting. Old pots may hold moisture, mold spores, or other elements that will cause the paint to peel.

2. **Determine your stripe width** by measuring the top of the pot just under the rim and dividing it into an even number of stripes. Make a small pencil mark at each side of each stripe. Make corresponding marks on the bottom edge of the pot. The stripe width will remain the same, but the spacing between the stripes will get smaller toward the bottom of the pot.

3. **Paint the stripes onto the pot using long,** even strokes. See photograph A. If necessary, apply a second coat of paint after the first one dries. The pot may soak up the paint, making several coats necessary.

4. **Paint the rim and upper edge of the pot.** See photograph B. Apply additional coats of paint if needed.

5. **After the paint dries,** brush on two or more coats of acrylic sealer or fixative. Let the pots dry at least 24 hours before planting. ❯**TIP** If you have trouble getting the lines straight and smooth and don't like an uneven, hand-painted look, try one of these two tricks:

1. **Use a disposable foam brush.** Foam brushes often leave a cleaner edge than bristle brushes.

2. **Run a line of narrow low-tack painter's tape** from the top mark to the corresponding bottom mark. Pull the tape straight and tight and seal it to the pot with an old credit card. Repeat for both edges of each of the stripes. Remove the tape after the paint dries.

You'll Need
❯*New terra-cotta clay pots*
❯*Sandpaper*
❯*Clean, lint-free rags*
❯*Tape measure*
❯*Pencil*
❯*Enamel paint in the desired color*
❯*Paintbrushes*
❯*Acrylic sealer or fixative*

❯**TIP** Letters and numbers are fun for plants in a children's garden or playroom, dots are a great mix with stripes, and squiggles remind you of giggles. Shaped sponges and stamps may give a more uneven texture than brushing on paint. Leave the bubble texture or use the stamped shape as a guide and paint over the design with a brush to make it more even.

This metal planter had great lines from the start, but the addition of leaves and stones sets it apart from all the others. Leaves glued and sealed to its surface add color and interest. If fall leaves aren't available when you are doing this project, purchase preserved leaves at floral supply or crafts stores or look for paper leaves at stationery stores or gourmet shops. (They are sometimes called cheese leaves because they were originally used as a plate liner under a cheese platter.) Stones dangle from the pot edge like pendants and are topped with natural-looking beads.

decoupage
&dangles

You'll Need
>*Galvanized pot with a flat rim*
>*Awl*
>*Hammer*
>*Fresh, preserved, or paper leaves*
>*Newspapers or kraft paper*
>*Rubber cement*
>*Soft cloth*
>*Clear sealer*
>*Paintbrush*
>*Copper wire*
>*Wire cutters (also called diagonal cutting pliers)*
>*Stones*
>*Needle-nose pliers*
>*Beads with holes large enough to receive the copper wire*

1. **Using an awl and hammer,** punch holes for the wire in the rim of the pot. Space the holes evenly and leave enough space between them for the stones to dangle.

2. **Lay the leaves right side down on the newspaper.** Coat each leaf with rubber cement. Press the leaves to the pot, overlapping them slightly. Rub the leaves with a soft cloth to affix them to the surface. After the pot is covered, coat it with two or more coats of sealer, making sure all the edges are tightly sealed.

3. **Cut copper wire** approximately three times the final desired length. Wrap a wire around a stone to hold it securely in a "cage", leaving a 1 inch tail. Complete your wrapping at the top of the stone. Using needle-nose pliers, wrap the tail around the remainder of the wire. See the photograph *opposite* for details. Crimp the final end against the long wire.

4. **Insert the remaining end up through a hole in the rim.** Slide one or more beads onto the wire. Adjust the length of the wire so the stone hangs where you want it, then bend the end of the wire back over the beads. Clip the end. See the photograph *opposite* for details. Repeat for the other holes.

Let the sound of bubbling water mask the noises of the world and bring calmness to your garden. Submersible pumps, available at crafts and home improvement stores, come in a variety of sizes and may have extras like variable speeds, adjustable heights, or even lights. Make sure the pump you choose is safe for outdoor use (some are designed for indoor use only). Check the pump label for suggested pot sizes and make sure the hole in the bottom of the pot is large enough for the cord to slip through. Have an electrician verify that your outdoor outlet has a ground fault circuit interrupter.

flowerpotfountain

1. Pull the pump cord through the bottom of the pot. If the drainage hole in the pot is too small, carefully enlarge it with a file. Leave several inches of cord on the inside of the pot. See photograph A for details.

2. Working from both the inside and the outside, fill the drainage hole with quick-drying cement compound. For the best results, use a putty knife. Make sure the hole is tightly sealed around the cord. See photograph B. Let the cement dry thoroughly and test the pot to make sure it is watertight. Add more cement if needed.

3. Coat the inside of the pot with liquid water sealant. See photograph C. Allow the sealant to dry so the pot is watertight.

4. Put the pot in place. Elevate it slightly on small pieces of paver brick or purchased pot feet. This will allow the cord to run under the pot and let the pot sit level.

5. Place several small bricks inside the pot and place the pump on the bricks. The top of the pump should be a few inches below the desired final water level for the fountain.

6. Assemble and install the pump according to the manufacturer's directions. Fill the pot with water to the desired level. Adjust the height of the pump as needed. ❯**NOTE** Unplug the pump when working with it. In cold climates, drain the pot and cover it during the winter. Freezing water may crack the pot and damage the pump.

❯**TIP** The water in the fountain may attract mosquitoes. Stock your pot with a few goldfish (they will eat the mosquito larvae) or use a chemical ring designed for small fountains and ponds.

You'll Need
❯*Large clay pot (at least 30 inches in diameter for most pumps)*
❯*Submersible pump*
❯*File (optional)*
❯*Quick-drying cement compound*
❯*Putty knife*
❯*Work gloves*
❯*Water sealant for unglazed tile or other porous surfaces*
❯*Paintbrush*
❯*Small concrete paver bricks or pot feet*
❯*Several small bricks*

A

B

C

tabletoptopiary

Have a ball shaping well-mannered topiaries from standard garden herbs and plants. Whether done singly or in a series, tabletop topiaries create elegant centerpieces indoors and out. Start with a healthy plant and an appropriately sized pot. Stake and trim the plant as it grows. Spheres are the most common topiary shape, but double and triple spheres, cones, or even cylinders work well for most plants. Follow the soil, watering, and feeding instructions for that plant.

You'll Need
❯*Herb or ornamental plant*
❯*Pot*
❯*Potting soil*
❯*Pruning shears or garden scissors*
❯*Straight twig, small bamboo stake, or garden stake*
❯*Raffia*

1. Transplant a healthy plant into the pot. Look for plants that have a single sturdy stem and sufficient fullness, especially toward the top.

2. Clip away the lower ancillary branches, leaving the lower two-thirds of the stem bare. See photograph A for details. If desired, a small cluster may be left at the base of the stem as shown for the plant on the table *above right*.

3. Insert a stake deeply into the pot. Using raffia, tie the stem of the topiary to the stake.

4. Trim the top shoot of the plant to encourage the plant to fill out on the sides rather than to continue growing straight up. See photograph B.

5. As the plant grows and fills out, prune it into the desired shape. Turn it weekly to encourage even growth. Once the desired shape and size are reached, continue trimming excess growth.

6. Periodically remove the ties to see if the topiary can stand without the stake.

Topiary Plants

The following plants work well for topiaries. Plants with a sturdy stem can be staked and shaped without a form. Vining plants may benefit from the use of a wire topiary form. Simply wind the plant around the form as it grows. Check garden supply stores for these and other plants that are sold in topiary form, then purchase similar plants to shape your own topiaries.
❯Rosemary ❯Lavender ❯Small Ivy ❯Myrtle
❯Bay ❯Angel Vine ❯Creeping Fig

A

B

Climbing vines are one of the hottest trends in garden plantings, and they don't have to be limited to trellises. Plant climbers like golden hops, ivy, morning glories, trumpet vine, cardinal climber, and nasturtium vine in large pots and give them a wire form for climbing. The tall tower shown opposite is made from inexpensive tomato cages. For interest, mix two different plants, making sure their light and water needs are compatible. The bright colors will add a focal point to your garden and the lush foliage creates privacy or blocks less than spectacular views.

bloomingtopiary

You'll Need
❭*Two metal coat hangers*
❭*Wire clippers*
❭*Large round pot*
❭*Two tomato cages*
❭*Pliers*
❭*Rocks, gravel, or shards of old pots*
❭*Potting soil*
❭*Plants (golden hops and blue morning glories were used here)*
❭*Wire or twine*

1. Clip each coat hanger near the hanging hook. Straighten out the hangers but not the hooks. Place the hangers in the pot. Bend the straight ends so that the hooks fall just below the upper edge of the pot. Leave as much wire across the bottom of the pot as possible to help anchor the hangers. Place rocks, gravel, or shards of old broken pots in the bottom of the pot. This will help with drainage and aid in keeping the coat hangers in place.

2. Fill the pot with potting soil so it is even with the top of the pot and the upper curve of the coat hanger hooks. Plant a golden hops plant on each side of the pot. See photograph A.

3. Slide one tomato cage, upside down, over the pot and plants. The upper ring should rest on the soil. See photograph B.

4. Turn the second cage one quarter-turn and slide it over the first cage. Push the cages into the soil slightly. Loop the hooks over the widest ring of the cages and pinch them over the ring using the pliers. This will help keep the form from blowing over on windy days.

5. Gather the spiked ends of the cages and wrap them together with wire or twine. Bend the upper ends tightly back on themselves to prevent them from scratching passers by or admirers.

6. Reach through the cages and plant morning glories in the remaining spaces. As the plants grow, wind them around the tomato cage wires. See photograph C. Pinch back the plants so they become fuller and less spindly.

For a completely organic look, turn to moss. Wire-framed planters and hanging baskets lined with sheet moss have a natural, neutral appearance that lets the plants take the spotlight. Flowers and foliage planted directly into a moss container tend to dry out very quickly and may need water at least once a day. Help the plants retain their moisture by keeping them in their plastic grower's pots.

moss-linedplanters

1. **Soak one sheet of moss in a bucket of water** for about 1 minute. Carefully wring the moss until it is damp-dry. Try to keep the moss from breaking apart. Starting at the back of the planter, press the moss into the wire frame. See photograph A.

2. **Soak and add a second sheet of moss.** Trim it as necessary. Where the pieces join, let them overlap. Use spray adhesive to join the pieces and make sure they fit the frame tightly. See photograph B.

3. **Arrange an assortment of potted herbs or flowers in the basket.** See photograph C. Turn some of the containers so the plants fall over the side or splay out at interesting angles. **›TIP** Place trailing plants in the front so they cascade over the rim of the planter as they grow. Use tall spiky plants to create a backdrop, and fill the remainder with medium-height plants of various colors and textures. If desired, place dirt between the pots to help hold them in place and further retain moisture. Potting soil designed to hold moisture works especially well. Once the arrangement is complete, cut or tear bits of moss to cover the top of the planter and conceal the pots. Water and spritz the plants often. **›TIP** If you are allergic to mold, take care when working with moss. It may contain mold spores, especially when wet. Wear a mask designed for allergies and plastic gloves.

You'll Need
›*Sheet moss*
›*Large bucket or basin for soaking moss*
›*Wire container*
›*Heavy-duty scissors (optional)*
›*Spray adhesive*
›*Various plants in 2- to 3-inch plastic grower's pots*

This little glass-encased landscape couldn't be easier to make or maintain. The only living plant is the moss. Purchase moss from the florist or gather it from your own property. When using live moss, keep a minimal amount of soil under the moss so it holds together. Live moss may not survive indoors for extended periods of time, even though the humidity of a terrarium and frequent misting help keep it moist. For a more permanent centerpiece, substitute green sheet moss. Add rocks, pieces of bark, pinecones, seashells, and twigs to complete your little portable oasis.

cakedometerrarium

You'll Need
❯Moss gathered from near streams or woods or sheet moss purchased at floral supply and crafts stores
❯Spade or shovel for digging moss (optional)
❯Bucket or basin for soaking sheet moss
❯Domed clear-glass cake stand
❯Stones, pebbles, bark, seashells, pinecones, twigs, or other small natural items
❯Spray bottle filled with water

1. If using fresh moss, carefully dig it up so a small amount of soil remains to hold it in a sheet. Do not dig moss from public areas. If using purchased sheet moss, soak it in water for about one hour, then wring it damp-dry.

2. Place the moss on the cake stand, mounding it slightly to create the look of a rolling landscape. See photograph A. Tuck it under at the edges so the underside doesn't show. Leave enough space at the edges to accommodate the dome.

3. Place stones, seashells, pinecones, and other elements of nature on the moss. Reshape the moss as needed to hold the decorative items. See photograph B.

4. Heavily mist the arrangement with water. See photograph C. Cover the arrangement with the dome. If moisture condenses on the inside of the dome, let it air out for a few hours. Spritz it with water every week or when the moss begins to look dry.

grassypastures

Here's the true definition of a low-maintenance lawn— grass grown in pots. No matter how hard the cold winds of winter are blowing, spring seems just around the corner with a centerpiece of terra-cotta pots and planters filled with sprouts of grass. At Easter, lay a few gaily decorated eggs among the blades. In the summer, place a fresh flower in a water-filled florist's vial and tuck it into the dirt or add miniature flags.

1. **If the pots have drainage holes,** cut small pieces of screen to cover the holes. This will prevent the dirt from washing through when the pot is watered. Add a layer of gravel or shards of broken pots to help with drainage.

2. **Fill the pots with potting soil.** Sow grass on top of the soil. Water the seed well using a gentle sprinkle from a watering can or the kitchen sink.

3. **Place the pots in a bright location.** Water as soon as the soil begins to look dry. Within two to three weeks, grass should start to grow. Trim the grass with scissors as needed.

❯**TIP** Start a new batch of grass every two to three weeks for a constant supply of spring-fresh centerpieces.

You'll Need
❯*Clay pots and planters*
❯*Small scrap of fiberglass screen (optional)*
❯*Scissors*
❯*Gravel or shards of broken pots*
❯*Potting soil (container mix that includes peat works well)*
❯*Annual grass seed such as rye*

When an item has outlived its original use, let it spend its retirement years in the sun. Old furniture, architectural salvage, toys that no longer hold their appeal, or old garden tools take on a new purpose when moved to the garden.

*quick**tricks**

Can Do Arrange a bouquet of freshly cut flowers in an old watering can or, if the can has a few leaks, use it as a container for potted plants. The leaks will serve as drainage holes. Old cans, tins, washtubs, buckets, and basins also are perfect for plantings. Use an awl and hammer to punch drainage holes in the bottom of the container. Add a layer of gravel to provide drainage and prevent the roots from getting soggy. Plant your favorite annuals in the proper potting soil and feed and water them as directed on their labels. For the most appeal, match the color of the flowers to a color on the container and make sure the plant will be slightly larger than its pot when in full bloom.

architecture
garden

Post It Newel posts from an architectural salvage yard serve a dual purpose in the garden. Their interesting shapes and intriguing textures act as sculpture, adding dimension to the plantings. As flowers grow taller, the posts can act as stakes and windbreaks. Use raffia or twine to tie spindly flowers upright, keeping the look natural and neutral. Tall posts will need to be buried several inches in the soil to keep them from tipping. Seal the portion that will be underground with several coats of sealer. Dig a hole, set the post in place, and pack the dirt back around it. If the post needs to be stabilized but isn't tall enough to have several inches buried, purchase four garden stakes. Paint the stakes to match the post and nail them to the lower section of the post. Pound the stakes into the ground. The surrounding plants will cover the overlap as they grow.

Pull Up a Chair The caned seat of this chair wore away, but the frame still had loads of appeal. Give an old chair a place of honor in the garden and plant tall flowers to grow up through the seat area. The frame of the chair will keep the flowers from falling over as they grow. Before placing the chair in the garden, give it two or more coats of matte-finish marine varnish to protect it from the elements. Be sure to move it inside for the winter in cold climates, or weather changes may loosen the joints.

Toy with It An old wagon takes a rest in a flower patch. Here a wooden goat cart holds pots of mixed flowers and foliage, elevating them to the focal point of a country garden. Old metal wagons, often available at curbside on trash day or for a few dollars at garage sales, work as well. For smaller plantings that can be used in beds or as a centerpiece, look for painted metal sand buckets, old toy pickup trucks, doll beds, or aging baby buggies and strollers. To protect the toys from rain and sun, spray them with two or more coats of matte or satin sealer. Placing the plants in pots instead of planting them directly in the toy also will keep the toys from rusting or rotting. Move them inside for the winter.

Garden-style decorating transcends the seasons and brings the freshness of spring and the warmth of summer to your home all year long. Just as a stroll through the garden calms the soul, time spent in a garden room beckons you to slow down, contemplate the day, and dream a bit. **This chapter tells you how to pull it all together,**

livin' the garden life

mix in patterns and colors, create focal points, and make the most of one or two spectacular pieces. Don't limit yourself to a single idea or item. Just as gardeners are quick to try a new rose, garden-style decorators rejoice when a new item shows up at a flea market or garden center. **Weeding out the old and bringing in the new keep your room fresh as a daisy.**

A room filled with delicate floral patterns brings to mind an English flower garden. A grid of botanical prints creates the focal point of this garden room much as a rose garden may be the focal point of a traditional British yard.

flowerpower

Ruffled slipcovers and pillows, lace table-cloths, and painted furniture establish cottage-style comfort, but for a dressier version of the style, keep fabrics, walls, and even furnishings in shades of creamy white. For color, let a grid of botanical prints take center stage. Old or reproduction botanical books often have pages and prints worthy of framing. Watch flea markets for old books and check out discount booksellers for low-cost volumes. Also check museum shops and art stores for collections of prints. Displaying the prints in identical frames that match the wall color emphasizes the hues in the prints and focuses attention on the subject matter. Hanging the prints in an orderly grid creates a formal effect. Floral pillows and a lampshade with additional botanical prints bring the floral motifs from the wall into the room. This kind of repetition is important for creating unity, knitting the wall art into the room's decoration.

Pair floral patterns with jaunty checks or sleek stripes to create spaces that feel fun, fresh, and much less formal than their all-blooming counterparts. The classic checks shown here with their bold colors and clean lines bring to mind summer picnics and give a dining area a casual, relaxed look. Both vintage and reproduction fabrics are used in the pillows, Roman shades, slipcovers, and tablecloths for a room that is practical as well as nostalgic.

adding geometrics

Layering the fabrics (a small floral cloth draped over a larger gingham one and a rose-blossom pillow on a checked chair) adds vibrancy to the room. A neutral background keeps the area from looking cluttered and jittery.

To successfully mix florals and geometrics, make sure they share some common ground. In the room shown *opposite*, the color red holds it all together. The blue cloth adds cooling contrast, but red is the mainstay. The fabrics are of similar weight and texture and have a casual, relaxed look. Florals dominate—there are three floral designs and only one check in several sizes. When mixing patterns, letting one type of pattern be the star makes the room look planned, not haphazard. Covering the chairs with generous slipcovers and the table with a long cloth keeps the focus on the fabric patterns and hides structural lines that might confuse the eye.

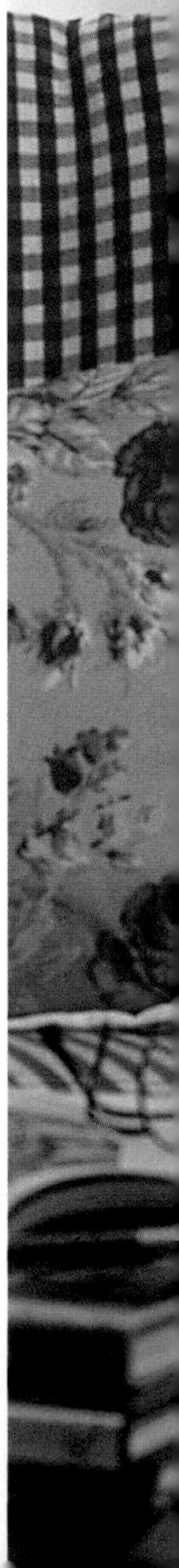

Go ahead—count them. There are at least 15 patterns in this small corner of a room. There are a few tricks to carrying off such a mixture with panache.

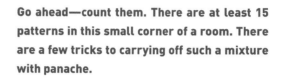

the **layered** look

Many of the patterns are consolidated in one small area. For example, the wing chair sports five patterns plus one more on the pillow. By confining these patterns to one item instead of spreading them across the room, they are visually controlled. It's like putting a fence around a frenzy of wildflowers so they don't take over the whole meadow. The same theory applies to the sofa and its mismatched pillows. Each acts almost like a separate miniature flower bed. The checked window curtains offer some relief from the floral patterns. Keeping the print the same even when the color differs creates unity.

⟩TIP Large expanses of plain spaces bring visual relief to the room and help calm the riot of patterns. Big open windows, plain wainscoting, a solid-color table and bench, a neutral rug, and sparsely patterned wallpaper bring calm to the overall appearance of the room. (See page 63 for instructions on making the valances.)

Garden architecture tends to be bold and oversized so it isn't overlooked in the great outdoors. When brought indoors, it makes an even stronger statement. Old artifacts, new pieces, and reproductions made to look aged work together well when each has enough integrity to stand on its own. Keep scale in mind so one item doesn't overpower the rest.

study architecture

Here the armillary sphere is elevated on a pedestal to give it more emphasis in relationship to the heavier urn and finials. Because these pieces have similar aged and rustic finishes, they present a unified look when put together.

A neutral background lets the pieces assume a sense of importance much the way a plain backdrop showcases paintings in a museum. Solid white walls, unadorned windows, a neutral floor, and clean-lined furniture upholstered in simple checks add interest but don't compete with the main pieces.

Look for new or reproduction pieces at antiques fairs, flea markets, roadside stands, and import shops. Ask about any finish that has been applied. Many have a heavy coat of lacquer that will retard rust on pieces left outdoors. If you want a rusted look, ask for items without this finish. To speed the rusting process, leave the item outdoors and periodically spray it with salt water. To prevent the rust from rubbing off once the item is brought indoors, give it two light coats of spray sealer. **>TIP** Many inexpensive imported reproductions have not been handled carefully. Check that the item is in good shape, sits level, and has solid joints and seams.

The garden design here is more subtle and in keeping with the Mission style of the house. The simple, straight lines of the Adirondack chairs, the wash bench coffee table, and the fencerow above the fireplace complement the unadorned lines of the home. Plants, a floral slipcover, and garden-print pillows keep the room from looking hard and uncomfortable.

garden style withamission

The first step in transforming this room was to sponge-paint the white-brick fireplace with glazes in varying shades of green. Now the brick resembles the velvety texture and color variations of moss. This blends the fireplace more harmoniously with the woodwork. Pale green paint on the walls underscores the garden-fresh look.

A loose-fitting floral slipcover dresses up an old sofa. Draperies in the same colors reinforce the light, natural color scheme. Adirondack chairs come in from outdoors for easy-care seating. A soft pillow for back support adds comfort and a contrasting color accent.

Finally, a section of picket fence attached to the wall over the fireplace brings the garden theme indoors. Decorated with garden tools and artwork and "planted" with a foreground of potted plants, it makes a fun focal point for the room.

A garden-style entryway provides the perfect transition between the yard and house. An outdoor bench piled with vintage pillows not only sets the stage but also comes in handy for guests slipping boots and coats on and off. Ornate detailing in the metalwork wallpiece holding classic straw hats *left* and the classic stair rail *opposite* mimic a Victorian garden gate or fencerow.

enter here

Old wood or wire garden benches can often be found at antiques fairs and shops or flea markets. Garden supply stores, gardening catalogs, and the outdoor living section of department stores also carry outdoor benches. If you plan to paint the bench, go with a piece made of inexpensive unfinished wood or one that has been previously painted. Do not invest in expensive woods like teak and then paint over them.

If benches are not available, consider a row of old wooden folding chairs that were often used at church picnics and outdoor revival services. Two or three metal garden chairs would also serve the same purpose. Rugs made of rags, sisal, coir, or other natural materials favor the natural look.

sunnydelights

An enclosed porch becomes a restful retreat when decorated in colors and materials that reflect its lightness and brightness. A porch swing piled with colorful pillows sets the carefree tone for the room. Who can resist gently swaying the afternoon away?

For privacy, sheer panels cover most of the windows but still let the sunlight in. Glass vases topped with a precut glass tabletop add sparkle and practicality. Other reminders of the outdoors are hanging torches, plants, and a sisal rug. A retro-style fan is added for fun and to mimic a summer breeze on muggy days.

If a porch swing isn't practical for your space, consider an old glider, a pair of rockers, or even a hammock. Oversize glass vases may be hard to find, so consider large terra-cotta pots or oversized urns instead. Using a standard-size precut glass tabletop (available at decorating and import stores) often saves money over custom-cut pieces.

The whole point is to make the room as light and carefree as possible. Keep the colors clean and bright, simplify the accessories, and add a few touches of whimsy.

One fabulous accessory is often all it takes to make a grand statement in a small space. As tempting as it may be to employ a nautical or celestial theme when a sphere used by sailors and astronomers is the focal point, the piece has more impact when it is allowed to stand on its own merit.

makeapoint

Here an armillary sphere commands attention as soon as you enter the room. The matelassé upholstery and fade-away background guarantee that the sphere will be the first thing noticed. A rustic twig table and a few other garden accessories are subtle enough to draw attention toward, instead of away from, the sphere. Note that the accessories (table, vases, turtle, and granite balls) mimic the round shape of the sphere.

Whether your focal point is a major investment or a lucky find, ensure that it gets the attention it deserves. Although this sphere is large, its openness and delicate shape would easily be lost in a room full of pattern. When using items with airy shapes, keep your background as neutral as possible.

Go ahead—be a show-off. Gather some of your favorite things and place them out for viewing in a creative manner. Scout flea markets, antiques shows and shops, and architectural salvage spots for pieces similar to the ones shown here.

*quick**tricks**

Table Grace The main task for this rustic desk is to display odds and ends collected over the years. An old birdcage, a window frame, and pieces of folk art work together nicely when they share textures, colors, or shapes. Exposed studs divide the room into segments, each perfect for a different theme or set of collectibles. Strips of molding or painted stripes achieve a similar effect.

Glass Houses Miniature glass houses recall the Victorian passion for gardening year-round. Look for reproduction greenhouses at garden centers, in catalogs, or at home

ways to display

decorating shops. Fill them with pots of summer flowers in warm weather; with mums, pumpkins, and leaves in the fall; with poinsettias come winter; and with forced bulbs as spring approaches. They also provide a good home for fragile or antique collectibles such as figurines, dolls, old toys, or candlesticks.

Gate Keeper Banish the bulletin board. Let an old gate hold your favorite mementos and reminders. Clean up an old wire garden gate or section of fence and prop it against the wall. If it won't stay in place, mount a picture hook at the top of the gate to keep the upper edge in place. Paint the hook to match the wall so it will not be noticed. Scoot one or two heavier items against the bottom rail to keep the gate from slipping across the table.

Barrel of Fun Use large baskets, barrels, or carts to display garden tools, pots, and other outdoor accessories. Mount the basket on the wall, securing it to wall studs for security. Arrange old garden tools and items in the basket, holding them in place, if necessary, by using heavy floral wire. Tuck in silk foliage for softness and to fill up empty spaces.

To learn about materials, terms, techniques, or tools, check the following list of definitions. You'll also find tips to make your work easier.

intheknow

Glossary

> Antiquing: a technique to make new paint look old by adding a darker tint over the finished project. A thinned umber or brown glaze is brushed over dried paint and then wiped away, leaving behind darker streaks and smudges.

> Armillary sphere: a sphere- and arrow-shaped device used by ancient astrologers and sailors to show the position of important circles of celestial space as a way of tracking location and time. Also called an armillary sundial.

> Countersink: to position the head of a nail or screw flush to the surface. A countersink bit or awl is generally used.

> Crackle finish: also called alligator finish. The surface of an object has the appearance of aging, cracked paint. The base color shows through between the cracks. Commercial crackle mediums are available in the paint sections of many stores.

> Double-action hinge: a type of hinge that allows the door or panel to bend both ways.

> Finial: a decorative topper for a fence post, newel post, or other architectural item.

> Florist's foam: dense green foam with a soft texture and great absorbency and water-retention capabilities. Florist's foam is designed to hold flower stems, vials, or picks. When soaked in water, it stays moist to keep flowers fresh. Also called Oasis®.

> Florist's vial: a small plastic vial with a tight-fitting cap. The cap has a hole or X for inserting flower stems.

> Florist's wire: various gauges of wire used by florists to secure one item to another. Florist's wire comes either in strands or wrapped around a paddle. The larger the gauge number, the finer the wire.

> Glaze: a sheer medium that is mixed with paint to make it more translucent. Glaze also retards the drying of the paint, allowing more time for manipulating the paint for special techniques. Glaze is available in oil- and water-based formulas.

Match the glaze to the paint and use the same brand if possible.
> **Matelassé:** a heavy cotton fabric, usually white, that is constructed of a double layer of cloth quilted together to form a raised, puckered pattern.
> **Mission style:** an architectural style using heavy, plain lines. Oak is the most common wood used in Mission-style furniture and homes.
> **Newel post:** the large post at the head or base of a staircase.
> **Paper-wrapped floral wire:** florist's wire that has been wrapped with a tacky crepe-like paper. The wrapping helps conceal the wire in places where it may be visible. Paper-wrapped florist's wire is generally brown, green, or white.
> **Stencil plastic:** a rigid but flexible plastic for cutting stencils. Clear or frosted plastic is the easiest to use because you can see through it for placement. **>TIP** When cutting a stencil, if your knife slips and makes an unwanted slit, tape over the slit on the top side of the stencil. This will prevent paint from leaking through the slit. Taping the underside may allow paint to leak through to the back of the stencil.
> **Template:** a pattern that is cut out of a heavy paper or lightweight cardboard and traced around.
> **Wood cutouts:** shapes that are precut from thin wood. Some cutouts are flat shapes (circles, letters, bells) while others are thicker (blocks, balls, flowerpots). A few cutouts are flat on one side so they can be glued to another surface. For example, a flowerpot or ball shape may be cut in half so it can be glued to a picture frame or furnishings.

Paint Techniques

> **Aged finish:** layers of paint that make a new item look old. By removing parts of some layers, the lower layers will show through. A base coat is first applied. After it dries, the paint can be rubbed with wax to make the next coat easier to remove. (This step is optional). A second coat of paint in a contrasting color is then applied and allowed to dry. More coats can be added, depending on the number of colors you want to show through. After all the paint has dried, sand the piece to remove one layer of paint at a time. If several colors were used, stop at different points so all the layers show. Do the most sanding in areas that would have received the most wear—on the edges and corners, around knobs, near handles, or around spots where the piece would have been handled.
> **Antiqued finish:** a darker paint or glaze top coat used to make the new paint look older. After the initial painting, dilute brown or umber paint with water, glaze, or another appropriate thinner. Brush the dark paint over the new paint, working in small sections so the antiquing solution does not dry. Wipe away the excess paint. Streaks and brushstrokes may be left for a more weathered effect. If the antiquing is not dark enough, add another coat. Allow the antiquing solution to be darker in corners, around edges, and in recessed areas. Commercial antiquing liquid is available.
> **Crackle finish:** a finish where the top coat of paint pulls away and leaves cracks that show the underlying coats. Paint on the base coat and allow it to dry. Brush on a commercial crackle medium (available in the paint section of stores) according to the manufacturer's directions. Follow the directions carefully as they differ from brand to brand. Using long, even strokes, add the top coat according to the manufacturer's directions and allow it to crackle. The crackles will not show immediately. It is best to use a single coat of crackle medium and a single coat of top paint. Practice this technique on a scrap. The thickness of the crackle medium affects the size of the crackles.
> **Dry-brush finish:** a streaked or chalky effect created by applying a very small amount of paint with a dry brush. Dip the tips of a bristle brush into paint. Wipe the brush onto a paper plate or cardboard to remove almost all the paint. Lightly stroke the remaining paint onto the piece you are painting. If too much paint is applied, spread it out with a clean paintbrush.
> **Glazed finish:** a translucent color applied over the base coat to create a feeling of depth. Mix the paint and glaze to the desired proportions. See the directions on the glaze can for suggested proportions. Test the technique before applying it to walls or furniture and make necessary adjustments. Glaze may be applied to an entire wall or done in stripes to create a two-tone finish. To stripe a wall, tape off the area to be glazed with low-tack painter's tape. Apply glaze to the taped-off sections, let it dry, then remove the tape.
> **Rubbed finish:** an aged look created by a glaze that is rubbed over fresh paint. Dampen a clean, lint-free rag and wring it out. Dip it into the glaze mixture and rub it onto the painted piece. Let more paint accumulate in recessed areas and use less paint on raised areas or where the piece would have received more exposure and wear. This technique may be used in reverse if a heavier glaze coat is desired. Working in small sections, paint on the glaze. Use a dampened rag to remove it. The first technique is called rubbing on or positive rubbing. The second technique is called rubbing off or negative rubbing.

Tools

> **All-thread pipe:** a hollow pipe that is completely threaded on the outside so no matter how long or short it is cut, the ends will always be threaded. All-thread pipe is usually available in 2- and 3-foot lengths and various diameters. When used for a lamp, the most common size is an outside diameter of $3/8$ inch and an inside diameter of $1/8$ inch. **>TIP** When cutting all-thread pipe with a hacksaw, cut between two nuts. After the cut is made, twist the nuts over the cut to smooth off burrs.

> **Artist's brush:** a thin bristle brush like those used by artists. For the best results, use artist's brushes instead of children's brushes. The bristles will give a more even stroke and nicer finish and will lose fewer bristles.

> **Awl:** an ice pick-like tool with a round wooden handle, a metal shaft about 3 inches long, and a pointed end. Use an awl to start holes for nails or a drill bit. Place the awl point on the marked spot, gently tap it with a hammer to make a small pilot hole, and then use this hole to keep the nail or drill bit from slipping out of place as you work.

> **Countersink bit:** a mushroom-shaped drill bit that makes a beveled recessed hole to receive the screw head. This allows the screws to be completely flush with a wooden surface. Use flat-head screws in conjunction with a countersink bit.

> **Crafts knife:** a thin-bladed knife with a metal handle about the diameter of a pencil. The blades can easily be replaced by turning the head of the knife. Different styles of blades are available and some knives have pivoting heads.

> **Dust mask:** a face mask used for protection against dust or fumes. Be sure to read the label to make sure the mask is appropriate for what you will be doing. Always wear the appropriate mask when working with strong chemicals or sanding old paint that may contain lead.

> **Etching cream:** a cream-style acid that is painted on glass. It will eat away the shiny outer surface of the glass and leave a frosted finish. Available at crafts stores.

> **Fabric markers:** any of a number of pens, pencils, or chalk products that are made specifically for use on fabric. Chalk brushes away (a damp cloth may be needed). The pens and pencils either fade away over time or disappear when dampened.

> **Finish nail:** a thin nail with a very small head.

> **Low-tack painter's tape:** a quick-release tape that is used by painters instead of masking tape. It adheres well to the surface but removes easily without leaving sticky residue. **>TIP** To seal the tape to the surface, run a piece of rigid plastic (such as an old credit card) over the edges.

> **Mirror clips:** clear plastic clips that are used to hang frameless mirrors. One end of the clip fits against the wall and has a hole for a screw. A lip holds the mirror edge, and the remaining end overlaps the mirror to hold it in place.

> **Needle-nose pliers:** pliers with long, slender, tapered jaws. Needle-nose pliers are used for working in small or tight spaces and also can be used to hold a small nail in place when hammering it. Also called long-nose or thin-nose pliers.

> **Picture hook:** a small, thin metal strap with a triangular loop at one end and a V shape at the other end. A nail slides through holes in the upper loop, going into the wall at an angle. Check the packaging because different sizes will hold different weights. The package should also contain the proper-size nails for that picture hook.

> **Sandpaper (grades):** an abrasive paper used to smooth out rough surfaces. It comes in different grades or degrees of coarseness. Very fine=280–220 grit; Fine=180–150 grit; medium=120–80 grit; coarse=60–40 grit.

> **Sawtooth hanger:** a metal strip nailed or tacked to the back of a picture so it can hang from a nail. The upper edge of the strip is smooth but the lower edge has a zigzag appearance so the hanger will fit over a nail without sliding.

> **Self-healing mat:** a special rubber-like mat used for cutting. Originally designed for quilters using rotary cutters, these mats resist almost all damage made by blades and once a cut is made, the surface closes up.

> **Spray adhesive:** aerosol glue. Most manufacturers recommend that for the best results, both surfaces be lightly sprayed, the glue be allowed to dry until tacky, and then the two pieces be pressed together. Some spray adhesives are permanent on contact but others are repositionable, allowing you to pick up the piece and move it before the glue dries. Check the label before buying spray adhesive.

> **Stencil adhesive:** a repositionable spray glue made for adhering stencils to walls, ceilings, floors, or furniture. Spray the back of the stencil and allow the glue to dry until tacky. Press the stencil to the wall, paint the design, then peel the stencil away and move it to the next spot. No residue should remain. When finished, clean the glue off the stencil.

> **Stencil brush:** a brush with dense, straight-sided bristles made for stenciling. **>TIP** After you finish stenciling, place a little soap on your palm and rub the brush into the soap to remove the leftover paint. Rinse the brush thoroughly, then wrap rubber bands around the bristles so they maintain their compact shape.

> **Stencil paints:** acrylic paints made for stenciling. In liquid form, they are sometimes thicker than regular acrylic paint. Cream form is like shoe polish. Crayon form looks like a large crayon. Rub the crayon onto paper, then pick up the paint from the paper with a stencil brush. Regular acrylic paint can also be used, but thinner brands may seep under the surface of the stencil and give a jagged line to your design.

> **Tack cloth:** a cheesecloth-like fabric that is embedded with wax to help it pick up dust and other small particles.

> **Textile medium:** a liquid mixed with acrylic paints to make them more permanent and softer when applied to fabric. It is best to use the same brand of paint and textile medium.

> **Threaded rod:** see all-thread pipe.

> **Utility knife:** a large knife with a sturdy blade. Many utility knives use a razor blade.

> **Wire brush:** a brush with several rows of stiff wire bristles used for cleaning rough surfaces and removing flaking paint. **>TIP** Store wire brushes in a dry place so the bristles do not rust.

U.S. Units To Metric Equivalents			Metric Units To U.S. Equivalents		
To Convert From	Multiply By	To Get	To Convert From	Multiply By	To Get
Inches	25.4	Millimeters (mm)	Millimeters	0.0394	Inches
Inches	2.54	Centimeters (cm)	Centimeters	0.3937	Inches
Feet	30.48	Centimeters (cm)	Centimeters	0.0328	Feet
Feet	0.3048	Meters (m)	Meters	3.2808	Feet